Lean and Green Air Fryer Cookbook 2021

365-Days Easy & Tasty Air Fryer Recipes to Help You Staying Healthy and Make Weight Loss Easier

Barbara Veith

Table of Contents

Salad Recipes 74

Dessert Recipes 83

Conclusion 89

Introduction

The Lean and Green diet is a diet where the basic idea is to cut out junk food, eat only 'lean' meat, such as fish, poultry and vegetables and also drink a lot of green tea. This diet is said to be not only good for your health but also a good way to control weight. The diet claims to reduce your weight, as well as reducing the risk of gout and other diseases.

There have been many scientific studies on this diet over the years, which find that the diet can reduce excess weight, blood pressure and cholesterol levels.

The biggest advantage of this diet is that you do not need to count calories or anything like that. The diet is based on the concept that we only consume what we need in terms of calories – not more. The theory is that if you eat only a certain amount of food, your body will use its stored energy (fat) to convert the food into energy, so you will not gain weight.

Lean and Green is a concept which is very similar to the Atkins diet, but the main difference between Lean and Green and Atkins is that Lean and Green only allows you to eat foods which have a low glycemic index value.

The Glycemic Index (GI) is often used in scientific studies to determine how certain foods affect weight control. A food's GI value shows how much that food affects blood sugar levels. In the short term, this means that you can eat more of a low GI food than a high GI food. In the long term though, a diet high in low GI foods is healthier.

In the "Lean and green" diet, you are not allowed to eat any carbohydrates which have a GI value above 50. Also, you are not allowed to drink milk. This means that you can eat only fish, poultry and vegetables such as carrots and broccoli.

The main disadvantage of this diet is that it does not take into consideration your body type or physical constitution (i.e. whether you are ectomorphic or mesomorphic). The diet is good for anyone who wants to lose weight, but it is only a weight loss diet.

However, many people believe that this diet is more than just the best way to lose weight. The Lean and Green diet also aims to reduce the risk of several diseases and claims that it is a low-calorie diet. Although there are some studies suggesting that the diet reduces blood pressure and cholesterol levels, these claims have not been proven yet.

Lean and green diet has proven to be extremely helpful in controlling and maintaining weight. Still, when lean & green food merges with air frying, it can make this diet much easier for people to follow. Air frying food cuts the cooking time in half and makes the food more nutritious.

Air frying is an innovative heat cooking method that is gaining popularity in India. In practical terms, cooking is done without oil. Preparing food using methods like air frying along with lean and green foods, it can give better results.

With the advent of health-conscious people, more and more people are also turning into this diet to lose weight and remain healthy. Most people are already aware that the air fryer is a great and healthy way to prepare food, but it is not so popular to opt for.

The air fryer works by blasting a heating element and circulating heated air inside a rotating drum filled with the food that is being prepared.

This diet is commonly followed by people who are looking for a successful way to lose weight. The diet is different from all the other diets followed by people around the globe. This diet plan is a success story, a mind-boggling one.

Appetizer and Snack Recipes

Crispy Jalapeno Coins

Difficulty: Easy
Preparation Time: 10 minutes
Cooking Time: 5 minutes
Servings: 1
Ingredients:

- 1 egg (1 healthy fat)
- 2-3 Tbsp. coconut flour (1 healthy fat)
- 1 sliced and seeded jalapeno (2 greens)
- Pinch of garlic powder (1 condiment)
- Bit of Cajun seasoning (optional)
- Pinch of pepper and salt (1 condiment)

Directions:

1. Preparing the Ingredients. Ensure your Instant Crisp Air Fryer is preheated to 400 degrees.

2. Mix all dry ingredients.

3. Pat jalapeno slices dry. Dip coins into the egg wash and then into the dry mixture. Toss to coat thoroughly.

4. Add coated jalapeno slices to Instant Crisp Air Fryer in a singular layer. Spray with olive oil.

5. Lock the air fryer lid. Set temperature to 350°F and set time to 5 minutes. Cook just till crispy.

Nutrition:

- 128 Calories
- 8g Fat
- 7g Protein

Jalapeno Cheese Balls

Difficulty: Average
Preparation Time: 10 minutes
Cooking Time: 8 minutes
Servings: 1
Ingredients:

- 1 Ounce cream cheese (2 healthy fats)
- 1/6 Cup shredded mozzarella cheese (1/3 healthy fat)
- 1/6 Cup shredded Cheddar cheese (1/3 healthy fat)
- 1/2 Jalapeños, finely chopped (1 green)
- 1/2 Cup breadcrumbs (1 healthy fat)
- 2 eggs (4 healthy fats)
- 1/2 Cup all-purpose flour (1 healthy fat)
- Salt (1/2 condiment)
- Pepper (1/2 condiment)

Directions:

1. Combine the cream cheese, mozzarella, Cheddar, and jalapeños in a medium bowl. Mix well.

2. Form the cheese mixture into balls about an inch thick. You may also use a small ice cream scoop. It works well.

3. Arrange the cheese balls on a sheet pan and place in the freezer for 15 minutes. It will help the cheese balls maintain their shape while frying.

4. Spray the Instant Crisp Air Fryer basket with cooking oil. Place the breadcrumbs in a small bowl. In another small bowl, beat the eggs. In the third small bowl, combine the flour with salt and pepper to taste, and mix well. Remove the cheese balls from the freezer. Plunge the cheese balls in the flour, then the eggs, and then the breadcrumbs.

5. Place the cheese balls in the Instant Crisp Air Fryer. Spray with cooking oil. Lock the air fryer lid—Cook for 8 minutes.

6. Open the Instant Crisp Air Fryer and flip the cheese balls. I recommend flipping them instead of shaking, so the balls maintain their form. Cook an additional 4 minutes. Cool before serving.

Nutrition:

- 96 Calories
- 6g Fat
- 4g Protein

Air Fryer Asparagus

Difficulty: Easy
Preparation Time: 5 minutes
Cooking Time: 8 minutes
Servings: 1
Ingredients:

- Nutritional yeast (1 condiment)
- Olive oil non-stick spray (1 healthy fat)
- 1 bunch of asparagus (9 greens)

Directions:

1. Wash asparagus and do not forget to trim off the thick woody ends.

2. Spray asparagus with olive oil spray and sprinkle with yeast.

3. In your Instant Crisp Air Fryer, lay asparagus in a singular layer. Set the temperature to 360°F. While the time limit to 8 minutes.

Nutrition:

- 17 Calories
- 4g Fat
- 9g Protein

Buffalo Cauliflower

Difficulty: Difficult
Preparation Time: 5 minutes
Cooking Time: 15 minutes
Servings: 1
Ingredients:
Cauliflower:

- 1 Cup panko breadcrumbs (1 healthy fat)
- 1 Tsp. salt (1 condiment)
- 2 Cups cauliflower florets (2 greens)

Buffalo Coating:

- 1/4 Cup Vegan Buffalo sauce (1/2 condiment)
- 1/4 Cup melted vegan butter (1/2 healthy fat)

Directions:

1. Melt butter in microwave and whisk in buffalo sauce.

2. Dip each cauliflower floret into the buffalo mixture, ensuring it gets coated well. Holdover a bowl till the floret is done dripping.

3. Mix breadcrumbs with salt.

4. Dredge dipped florets into breadcrumbs and place them into Instant Crisp Air Fryer. Lock the air fryer lid. Set temperature to 350°F and set time to 15 minutes. When slightly browned, they are ready to eat!

5. Serve with your favorite Keto dipping sauce!

Nutrition:

- 194 Calories
- 17g Fat
- 10g Protein

Bell-Pepper Wrapped in Tortilla

Difficulty: Easy
Preparation Time: 5 minutes
Cooking Time: 15 minutes
Servings: 1
Ingredients:

- 1/4 Small red bell pepper (1/2 greens)
- 1/4 Tablespoon water (1/2 condiment)
- 1 large tortilla (1 healthy fat)
- 1-piece commercial vegan nuggets, chopped (3 leans)
- Mixed greens for garnish (6 greens)

Directions:

1. Preheat the Instant Crisp Air Fryer to 400°F.

2. In a skillet heated over medium heat, water sautés the vegan nuggets and bell peppers. Set aside.

3. Place filling inside the corn tortillas.

4. Fold the tortillas, place them inside the Instant Crisp Air Fryer, and cook for 15 minutes until the tortilla wraps are crispy.

5. Serve with mixed greens on top.

Nutrition:

- 548 Calories
- 21g Fat
- 46g Protein

Coconut Battered Cauliflower Bites

Difficulty: Average
Preparation Time: 5 minutes
Cooking Time: 20 minutes
Servings: 1
Ingredients:

- Salt and pepper to taste (2 condiments)
- 1 flax egg or one tablespoon flaxseed meal + 3 tablespoon water (1 healthy fat)
- 1 small cauliflower, cut into florets (2 greens)
- 1 teaspoon mixed spice (1 condiment)

- 1/2 teaspoon mustard powder (1 condiment)
- 2 tablespoons maple syrup (2 healthy fats)
- 1 clove of garlic, minced (1 green)
- 2 tablespoons soy sauce (2 condiments)
- 1/3 Cup oats flour (1/2 healthy fat)
- 1/3 Cup plain flour (1/2 healthy fat)
- 1/3 Cup desiccated coconut (1/2 lean)

Directions:

1. In a mixing bowl, mix oats, flour, and desiccated coconut. Season with salt and pepper to taste. Set aside.

2. In another bowl, place the flax egg and add a pinch of salt to taste. Set aside.

3. Season the cauliflower with mixed spice and mustard powder.

4. Dredge the florets in the flax egg first, then in the flour mixture.

5. Place inside the Instant Crisp Air Fryer, lock the air fryer lid and cook at 400°F or 15 minutes.

6. Meanwhile, place the maple syrup, garlic, and soy sauce in a saucepan and heat over medium flame. Wait for it to boil and adjust the heat to low until the sauce thickens.

7. After 15 minutes, take out the Instant Crisp Air Fryer's florets and place them in the saucepan.

8. Toss to coat the florets and place inside the Instant Crisp Air Fryer and cook for another 5 minutes.

Nutrition:

- 154 Calories
- 2.3g Fat
- 4.6g Protein

Avocado Fries

Difficulty: Easy

Preparation Time: 10 minutes

Cooking Time: 7 minutes

Servings: 1

Ingredients:

- 1 avocado (2 healthy fats)
- 1/8 tsp. salt (1/4 condiments)
- 1/4 Cup panko breadcrumbs (1/2 healthy fat)
- Bean liquid (aquafaba) a 15-ounce can of white or garbanzo beans (6 greens)

Directions:

1. Peel, pit, and slice up the avocado.

2. Toss salt and breadcrumbs together in a bowl. Place aquafaba into another bowl.

3. Dredge slices of avocado first in aquafaba and then in panko, making sure you can even coat them.

4. Place coated avocado slices into a single layer in the Instant Crisp Air Fryer. Set temperature to 390°F and set time to 5 minutes.

5. Serve with your favorite Keto dipping sauce!

Nutrition:

- 102 Calories
- 22g Fat
- 9g Protein

Slow Cooker Savory Butternut Squash Oatmeal

Difficulty: Difficult

Preparation Time: 15 minutes

Cooking Time: 6 to 8 hours

Servings: 1

Ingredients:

- 1/4 Cup steel-cut oats (1/2 healthy fat)
- 1/2 Cups cubed (1/2-inch pieces) peeled butternut squash (1 green)
- 3/4 Cups of water (1 healthy fat)
- 1/16 Cup unsweetened nondairy milk (1/8 healthy fat)
- 1/4 Tablespoon chia seed (1/2 healthy fat)
- 1/2 Teaspoons yellow (mellow) miso paste (1 condiment)
- 3/4 Teaspoons ground ginger (1 condiment)
- 1/4 Tablespoon sesame seed, toasted (1/2 healthy fat)
- 1/4 Tablespoon chopped scallion, green parts only (1 green)
- Shredded carrot, for serving (optional) (1 green)

Directions:

1. In a slow cooker, combine the oats, butternut squash, and water.

2. Cover the slow cooker and cook on low for 6 to 8 hours, or until the squash is fork-tender. Using a potato masher or heavy spoon, roughly mash the cooked butternut squash. Stir to combine with the oats.

3. Whisk together the milk, chia seeds, miso paste, and ginger to combine in a large bowl. Stir the mixture into the oats.

4. Top your oatmeal bowl with sesame seeds and scallion for more plant-based fiber, top with shredded carrot (if using).

Nutrition:

- 230 Calories
- 5g Fat
- 7g Protein

Crispy Cauliflowers

Difficulty: Easy

Preparation Time: 10 minutes

Cooking Time: 10 minutes

Servings: 4

Ingredients:

- 2 Cup cauliflower florets, diced (6 greens)
- 1/2 Cup almond flour (1 healthy fat)
- 1/2 Cup coconut flour (1 healthy fat)
- Salt and pepper to taste (1/2 condiment)
- 1 Tsp. mixed herbs (1 green)
- 1 Tsp. chives, chopped (1 green)
- 1 Egg (1 lean)
- 1 Tsp. cumin (1 condiment)
- 1/2 Tsp. garlic powder (1 condiment)
- 1 Cup water (1 condiment)
- Oil for frying (1 condiment)

Directions:

1. Combine the egg, salt, garlic, water, cumin, chives, mixed herbs, pepper, and flour in a mixing bowl.

2. Stir in the cauliflower to the mixture and then fry them in oil until they become golden in color.

3. Serve.

Nutrition:

- 3.3g Protein
- 10.4g Fat
- 259 Calories

Zucchini Parmesan Chips

Difficulty: Easy

Preparation Time: 10 minutes

Cooking Time: 8 minutes

Servings: 1

Ingredients:

- 1/2 Tsp. paprika (1 condiments)
- 1/2 Cup grated parmesan cheese (1 healthy fat)
- 1/2 Cup Italian breadcrumbs (1 healthy fat)
- 1 lightly beaten egg (2 healthy fats)
- 2 thinly sliced zucchinis (4 greens)

Directions:

1. Use a very sharp knife or mandolin slicer to slice zucchini as thinly as you can. Pat off extra moisture.

2. Beat egg with a pinch of pepper and salt and a bit of water.

3. Combine paprika, cheese, and breadcrumbs in a bowl.

4. Dip slices of zucchini into the egg mixture and then into the breadcrumb mixture. Press gently to coat.

5. Mist with olive oil cooking spray encrusted zucchini slices. Put into your Instant Crisp Air Fryer in a single layer. Latch the air fryer lid. Set temperature to 350°F and set time to 8 minutes.

6. Sprinkle with salt and serve with salsa.

Nutrition:

- 211 Calories
- 16g Fat
- 8g Protein

Zucchini Omelet

Difficulty: Easy

Preparation Time: 10 minutes

Cooking Time: 10 minutes

Servings: 1

Ingredients:

- 1/2 Teaspoon butter (1 healthy fat)
- 1/2 Zucchini, julienned (1 green)
- 1 egg (1 lean)
- 1/8 tsp. fresh basil, chopped (1/4 green)
- 1/8 tsp. red pepper flakes (1/4 green)

- Salted and newly ground black pepper to taste (1/2 condiment)

Directions:

1. Preheat the Instant Crisp Air Fryer to 355 degrees F.

2. Melt butter on medium heat using a skillet.

3. Add zucchini and cook for about 3-4 minutes.

4. In a bowl, add the eggs, basil, red pepper flakes, salt, and black pepper and beat well.

5. Add cooked zucchini and gently stir to combine.

6. Transfer the mixture into the Instant Crisp Air Fryer pan. Lock the air fryer lid.

7. Cook for about 10 minutes. Also, you may opt to wait until it is done thoroughly.

Nutrition:

- 281 Calories
- 21g Fat
- 9g Protein

Cheesy Cauliflower Fritters

Difficulty: Average

Preparation Time: 10 minutes

Cooking Time: 7 minutes

Servings: 1

Ingredients:

- 1/2 Cup chopped parsley (1 green)
- 1 Cup Italian breadcrumbs (2 healthy fats)
- 1/3 Cup shredded mozzarella cheese (1 healthy fat)
- 1/3 Cup shredded sharp cheddar cheese (1 healthy fat)
- 1 egg (1 healthy fat)
- 2 minced garlic cloves (2 greens)
- 3 chopped scallions (6 greens)
- 1 head of cauliflower (3 greens)

Directions:

1. Preparing the Ingredients. Cut the cauliflower up into florets. Wash well and pat dry. Place into a food processor and pulse 20-30 seconds till it looks like rice.

2. Place the cauliflower rice in a bowl and mix with pepper, salt, egg, cheeses, breadcrumbs, garlic, and scallions.

3. With hands, form 15 patties of the mixture and then add more breadcrumbs if needed.

4. With olive oil, spritz patties, and put the fitters into your Instant Crisp Air Fryer. Pile it in a single layer. Lock the air fryer lid. Set temperature to 390°F, and set time to 7 minutes, flipping after 7 minutes.

Nutrition:

- 209 Calories
- 17g Fat
- 6g Protein

Spiced Pumpkin Muffins

Difficulty: Average

Preparation Time: 15 minutes

Cooking Time: 20 minutes

Servings: 1

Ingredients:

- 1/6 Tablespoons ground flaxseed (1/4 healthy fat)
- 1/24 Cup of water (1/4 condiment)
- 1/8 Cups whole wheat flour (1/4 healthy fat)
- 1/6 Teaspoons baking powder (1/3 healthy fat)
- 5/6 Teaspoons ground cinnamon (1/4 condiment)
- 1/12 Teaspoon baking soda (1/8 condiment)
- 1/12 Teaspoon ground ginger (1/8 condiment)
- 1/16 Teaspoon ground nutmeg (1/8 condiment)
- 1/32 Teaspoon ground cloves (1/8 condiment)
- 1/6 Cup pumpkin puree (1/3 healthy fat)
- 1/12 Cup pure maple syrup (1/8 healthy fat)
- 1/24 Cup unsweetened applesauce (1/8 healthy fat)
- 1/24 Cup unsweetened nondairy milk (1/8 healthy fat)
- 1/2 Teaspoons vanilla extract (1 healthy fat)

Directions:

1.   Preheat the oven to 350°F. Line a 12-cup metal muffin pan with parchment paper liners or use a silicone muffin pan.

2.   First, mix the flaxseed and water in a large bowl and then keep it aside.

3.   In a medium bowl, stir together the flour, baking powder, cinnamon, baking soda, ginger, nutmeg, and cloves.

4.   In a medium bowl, stir up the maple syrup, pumpkin puree, applesauce, milk, and vanilla. Using a spatula, mix the wet ingredients with the dry ones.

5.   Fold the soaked flaxseed into the batter until evenly combined, but do not overmix the batter, or your muffins will become dense. Ladle the batter with a ½ cup per muffin into your prepared muffin pan.

6.   Bake for 18 to 20 minutes. Remove the muffins from the pan.

7.   Transfer to a wire rack for cooling.

8.   Store in an air-tight container at room temperature.

Nutrition:

- 115 Calories
- 1g Fat
- 3g Protein

Mini Zucchini Bites

Difficulty: Average
Preparation Time: 10 minutes
Cooking Time: 10 minutes
Servings: 6
Ingredients:

- 1 Zucchini, cut into thick circles (2 greens)
- 3 Cherry tomatoes, halved (6 greens)
- 1/2 Cup parmesan cheese, grated (1 healthy fat)
- Salt and pepper to taste (1 condiment)
- 1 Tsp. chives, chopped (1 green)

Directions:

1.   Preheat the oven to 390 degrees F.

2.   Add wax paper on a baking sheet.

3.   Arrange the zucchini pieces.

4.   Add the cherry halves to each zucchini slice.

5.   Add parmesan cheese, chives, and sprinkle with salt and pepper.

6.   Bake for 10 minutes. Serve.

Nutrition:

- 1g Fat
- 7.3g Protein
- 361 Calories

Carrot Cake Oatmeal

Difficulty: Easy
Preparation Time: 10 minutes
Cooking Time: 15 minutes
Servings: 1
Ingredients:

- 1/8 Cup pecans (1/4 healthy fat)
- 1/2 Cup finely shredded carrot (1 green)
- 1/4 Cup old-fashioned oats (1/2 healthy fat)
- 5/8 Cups unsweetened nondairy milk (1/4 healthy fat)
- 1/2 Tablespoon pure maple syrup (1 healthy fat)
- 1/2 Teaspoon ground cinnamon (1 condiment)
- 1/2 Teaspoon ground ginger (1 condiment)
- 1/8 Teaspoon ground nutmeg (1/4 condiment)
- 1 tablespoon chia seed (1 healthy fat)

Directions:

1.   Over medium-high heat in a skillet, toast the pecans for 3 to 4 minutes, often stirring, until browned and fragrant (watch closely, as they can burn quickly). Pour the pecans onto a cutting board and coarsely chop them. Set aside.

2.   Using an 8-quart pot at medium-high heat, combine the carrot, oats, milk, maple syrup, cinnamon, ginger, and nutmeg. When it is already boiling, reduce the heat to medium-low. Cook, uncovered, for 10 minutes, stirring occasionally.

3.   Stir in the chopped pecans and chia seeds. Serve immediately.

Nutrition:

- 307 Calories
- 17g Fat
- 7g Protein

Plant-Powered Pancakes

Difficulty: Easy

Preparation Time: 5 minutes

Cooking Time: 15 minutes

Servings: 8

Ingredients:

- 1 Cup whole-wheat flour (1 healthy fat)
- 1 Teaspoon baking powder (1/2 healthy fat)
- 1/2 Teaspoon ground cinnamon (1/2 condiment)
- 1 Cup plant-based milk (1 healthy fat)
- 1/2 Cup unsweetened applesauce (1 healthy fat)
- 1/4 Cup maple syrup (1/2 healthy fat)
- 1 Teaspoon vanilla extract (1 healthy fat)

Directions:

1. In a large bowl, combine the flour, baking powder, and cinnamon.

2. Stir in the milk, applesauce, maple syrup, and vanilla until no dry flour is left, and the batter is smooth.

3. Preheat a huge, non-stick skillet over medium heat. For each pancake, pour 1/4 cup of batter onto the hot skillet. Once bubbles form over the top of the pancake and the sides begin to brown, flip and cook for 1 to 2 minutes more.

4. Repeat until all of the batters are used and serve.

Nutrition:

- 2g Fat
- 5g Protein
- 591 Calories

Cauliflower Rice

Difficulty: Average

Preparation Time: 5 minutes

Cooking Time: 20 minutes

Servings: 1

Ingredients:

Round 1:

- 1/2 Tsp. turmeric (1 condiment)
- 1/2 Cup diced carrot (1 green)
- 1/2 Tbsp. low-sodium soy sauce (1 condiment)
- 1/8 Block of extra firm tofu (1/4 healthy fat)

Round 2:

- 1/4 minced garlic cloves (1/2 green)
- 1/2 Cup chopped broccoli (1 green)
- 1/2 Tbsp. minced ginger (1/2 green)
- 1/4 Tbsp. rice vinegar (1/2 condiment)
- 1/4 Tsp. toasted sesame oil (1/4 healthy fat)
- 1/2 Tbsp. reduced-sodium soy sauce (1 condiment)
- 1/2 Cup rice cauliflower (1 green)

Directions:

1. Crush tofu in a large bowl and toss with all the Round 1 ingredients.

2. Lock the air fryer lid—Preheat the Instant Crisp Air Fryer to 370 degrees. Also, set the temperature to 370°F, set the time to 10 minutes, and cook 10 minutes, making sure to shake once.

3. In another bowl, toss ingredients from Round 2 together.

4. Add Round 2 mixture to Instant Crisp Air Fryer and cook another 10 minutes to shake 5 minutes.

Nutrition:

- 67 Calories
- 8g Fat
- 3g Protein

Spiced Sorghum and Berries

Difficulty: Easy

Preparation Time: 5 minutes

Cooking Time: 1 hour

Servings: 1

Ingredients:

- 1/4 Cup whole-grain sorghum (1/2 healthy fat)
- ¼ tsp. ground cinnamon (1/2 condiment)
- 1/4 Teaspoon Chinese five-spice powder (1/2 condiment)
- 3/4 Cups water (1 condiment)
- 1/4 Cup nondairy milk, unsweetened (1/2 healthy fat)
- 1/4 Teaspoon vanilla extract (1/2 healthy fat)
- 1/2 Tablespoons pure maple syrup (1 healthy fat)

- 1/2 Tablespoon chia seed (1 healthy fat)
- 1/8 Cup sliced almonds (1/4 lean)
- 1/2 Cups fresh raspberries, divided (1 lean)

Directions:

1. Using a large pot over medium-high heat, stir together the sorghum, cinnamon, five-spice powder, and water. Wait for the water to a boil, cover the bank, and reduce the heat to medium-low. Cook for 1 hour, or until the sorghum is soft and chewy. If the sorghum grains are still hard, add another water cup and cook for 15 minutes more.

2. Using a glass measuring cup, whisk together the milk, vanilla, and maple syrup to blend. Add the mixture to the sorghum and the chia seeds, almonds, and 1 cup of raspberries. Gently stir to combine.

3. When serving, top with the remaining 1 cup of fresh raspberries.

Nutrition:

- 289 Calories
- 8g Fat
- 9g Protein

Crispy Roasted Broccoli

Difficulty: Easy

Preparation Time: 10 minutes

Cooking Time: 8 minutes

Servings: 1

Ingredients:

- 1/4 Tsp. Masala (1/2 condiment)
- 1/2 Tsp. red chili powder (1 condiment)
- 1/2 Tsp. salt (1 condiment)
- 1/4 Tsp. turmeric powder (1/2 condiment)
- 1 Tbsp. chickpea flour (1 healthy fat)
- 1 Tbsp. yogurt (2 healthy fats)
- 1/2 Pound broccoli (1 green)

Directions:

1. Cut broccoli up into florets. Immerse in a bowl of water with two teaspoons of salt for at least half an hour to remove impurities.

2. Take out broccoli florets from water and let drain. Wipe down thoroughly.

3. Mix all other ingredients to create a marinade.

4. Toss broccoli florets in the marinade. Cover and chill for 15-30 minutes.

5. Preheat the Instant Crisp Air Fryer to 390 degrees. Place marinated broccoli florets into the fryer, lock the air fryer lid, set the temperature to 350°F, and set the time to 10 minutes. Florets will be crispy when done.

Nutrition:

- 96 Calories
- 1.3g Fat
- 7g Protein

Sweet Cashew Cheese Spread

Difficulty: Easy

Preparation Time: 5 minutes

Cooking Time: 5 minutes

Servings: 10

Ingredients:

- Stevia (5 drops) (1/2 condiment)
- Cashews (2 cups, raw) (3 healthy fats)
- Water (1/2 cup) (1 condiment)

Directions:

1. Soak the cashews overnight in water.

2. Next, drain the excess water, then transfer cashews to a food processor.

3. Add in the stevia and the water.

4. Process until smooth.

5. Serve chilled. Enjoy.

Nutrition:

- 7g Fat
- 5.7g Protein
- 322 Calories

Breakfast Recipes

Brine & Spinach Egg Muffins Air Fried

Difficulty: Difficult
Preparation Time: 10 minutes
Cooking Time: 25 minutes
Servings: 2
Ingredients:

For Egg Muffin

- Eggs – 4 (2 healthy fat)
- Liquid egg whites – 1 cup (1/2 healthy fat)
- Greek yogurt, plain, low fat - ¼ cup (1/2 healthy fat)
- Salt - ¼ tsp (1/4 condiment)

For Brie, Spinach & Mushroom Mix

- Brie – 1 oz (1/2 green)
- Spinach, frozen, coarsely chopped – 5 oz (2 greens)
- Mushrooms, chopped – 1 cup. (1/2 green)

Directions:

1. Thaw the frozen spinach for 10 minutes.
2. Wash all the vegetables separately and pat dry.
3. Preheat the air fryer to 190°C.
4. In a large bowl, combine Greek yogurt, egg whites, eggs, cheese, and salt.
5. Add all the vegetables in the bowl mix and combine well.
6. Take 12 muffin tins and lightly spray with cooking oil.
7. Transfer the mixture evenly into the muffin tins.
8. Place them in the air fryer and bake for 25 minutes until the center portion becomes hard.
9. Do a toothpick test by inserting it in the center and check if it comes out clean.
10. Take it out from the air fryer and allow it to settle down the heat before serving.
11. Enjoy your muffin.

Nutrition:

- 278 Calories
- 13.1g Fat
- 33g Protein

Cheddar Herb Pizza Bites

Difficulty: Average
Preparation Time: 5 minutes
Cooking Time: 10 minutes
Servings: 2
Ingredients:

- Optavia Buttermilk Cheddar Herb Biscuit – 2 sachets (1 condiment)
- Almond milk, unsweetened - ½ cup (1/2 healthy fat)
- Olive oil – 1 tsp (1/2 condiment)
- Basil leaves, julienned - ½ cup (1/2 green)
- Mozzarella stick, cut into 6 small pieces – 2 oz. (1 healthy fat)
- Tomatoes, sliced – 1 medium (1 green)
- Balsamic vinegar – 1 tbsp (1/2 condiment)

Directions:

1. Preheat the air fryer to 230°C.
2. Combine the Buttermilk Cheddar Herb Biscuit, olive oil, and almond milk in a large bowl until they become a smooth paste.
3. Take 6 muffin tin and spray lightly with cooking oil.
4. Distribute the mixture evenly into the muffin tin.
5. Place the muffin tin on the air fryer grill tray, topped with mozzarella and sliced tomato.
6. Sprinkle basil on top and bake for 10 minutes, until the biscuit mixture becomes brown and cheese starts to bubble.
7. Drop balsamic vinegar on top before serving.

Nutrition:

- 203 Calories
- 7g Fat
- 13g Protein

Shrimp Stuffed in Eggplant with Cauliflower Rice

Difficulty: Average

Preparation Time: 10 minutes

Cooking Time: 33 minutes

Servings: 2

Ingredients:

- Eggplant, large – 1 (2 greens)
- Salt, divided - ¼ tsp. (1/4 condiment)
- Shrimp, peeled & deveined - ½ lb. (2 leans)
- Black pepper, ground - ¼ tsp (1/4 condiment)
- Cauliflower, riced – 1 cup (1 green)
- Scallion, without the head, finely chopped – 1 (1 green)
- Greek yogurt, plain, low fat - ¼ cup (1/2 lean)
- Parmesan cheese, shredded - ¼ cup (1/2 healthy fat)

Directions:

1. Wash eggplant and cut into 4 rounds.
2. Remove the flesh and make it into a cup shape.
3. Chop the flesh and keep it ready to use.
4. Rub inside with half portion of the salt.
5. Put in the air fryer grill tray and bake for 18 minutes at 230°C.
6. After baking, keep it aside.
7. Now season the shrimp with pepper and the remaining salt.
8. Place it in the air fryer grill tray and spray some cooking oil.
9. Broil it for 5 minutes by flipping sides halfway through the cooking, until it turns to pink.
10. After that, remove and keep it aside.
11. In the air fry tray, put the chopped eggplant flesh, cauliflower rice, scallions, and air fry or 3-4 minutes until they become tender.
12. Transfer the air fried veggies into a bowl and add the fried shrimps into it.
13. Add yogurt and combine to mix.
14. Now scoop the mix into the eggplant cup.
15. Top it with grated parmesan cheese.
16. Put it in the air fryer baking grill and bake for 15 minutes at 230°C.
17. Serve hot.

Nutrition:

- 269 Calories
- 5.9g Fat
- 33g Protein

Sweet Potato Pecan Muffins

Difficulty: Average

Preparation Time: 10 minutes

Cooking Time: 20 minutes

Servings: 2

Ingredients:

- Optavia Select Honey Sweet Potatoes – 2 sachets (1/2 condiment)
- Optavia Essential Spiced Gingerbread – 2 sachets (1/2 condiment)
- Water – 1 cup (1/2 condiment)
- Liquid egg substitute – 6 tbsp (3 healthy fat)
- Cashew milk, unsweetened - ¼ cup (1/2 healthy fat)
- Pumpkin pie spice - ½ tsp (1/4 condiment)
- Vanilla extract - ½ tsp (1/4 condiment)
- Baking powder - ½ tsp (1/4 condiment)
- Pecans, chopped - 1½ oz (2 healthy fats)

Directions:

1. Preheat the air fryer to 180°C.
2. Do the directions on the packet to make the Honey Sweet Potatoes.
3. Allow it to cool for some time.
4. Mix the prepared honey sweet potatoes and all the other ingredients, except the pecans.
5. Lightly spray the muffin pan and transfer the mix to the slots evenly.
6. Top it with chopped pecans.
7. Situate it in the air fryer tray and bake for 20 minutes.
8. Serve hot.

Nutrition:

- 383 Calories
- 21g Fat
- 15g Protein

Mini Pepper Nachos

Difficulty: Average
Preparation Time: 10 minutes
Cooking Time: 13 minutes
Servings: 2
Ingredients:

- Jalapeno pepper, diced - ¼ cup (1/2 green)
- Bell pepper, halved, cored – 12 nos. (2 greens)
- Chicken breast, canned in low sodium water – 6 oz (3 lean)
- Avocado, mashed – 3 oz (2 healthy fats)
- Greek yogurt, plain, low fat - ¼ cup (1/2 healthy fat)
- Cheddar cheese, low fat, divided – 1 cup (1/2 healthy fat)
- Chili powder - ½ tsp (1/2 condiment)
- Scallions, chopped - ¼ cup. (1/2 green)

Directions:

1. Drain the chicken thoroughly.
2. Put the diced jalapeno pepper in the air fryer tray and spray some cooking spray oil.
3. Air fry it at 200°C for 2-3 minutes until they become tender.
4. Transfer them to a large bowl, add chicken, yogurt, avocado, half portion of cheese, jalapeno, chili powder, and combine to mix.
5. In the air fryer tray, arrange the bell pepper and fill the chicken mixture.
6. Top them with the remaining cheese.
7. Bake it for 10 minutes until the cheese starts to melt.
8. Serve with garnished scallion.

Nutrition

- 457 Calories
- 18.5g Fat
- 40g Protein

Air Fried Chicken and Cauliflower Rice

Difficulty: Average
Preparation Time: 10 minutes
Cooking Time: 45 minutes
Servings: 2

Ingredients:

- Chicken breast, chopped – 9 oz (3 leans)
- Cauliflower, grated, cooked - 2½ cup (3 greens)
- Tomatoes, diced - ½ cup (1/2 green)
- Salsa - ¼ cup (1/4 condiment)
- Pepper - ¼ tsp (1/4 condiment)
- Salt - ¼ tsp (1/4 condiment)
- Garlic powder - ¼ tsp (1/4 condiment)
- Parmesan cheese, low fat, shredded – 1 cup (1/2 healthy fat)
- Taco seasoning, low sodium - ½ tsp (1/4 condiment)
- Olive oil – 1 tsp (1/2 healthy fat)

Directions:

1. Wash chicken and drain it thoroughly.
2. Rub taco seasoning with olive oil on the chicken breast.
3. Marinate it for 4 hours.
4. Set the air fryer temperature to 180°C.
5. After that, place it in the air fryer grill and broil for 20 minutes by flipping side halfway through.
6. Once the cooking is over, remove and keep it aside.
7. In an air fryer bowl, mix the grated cauliflower, salsa, pepper, salt, garlic powder, and tomatoes.
8. Transfer the broiled chicken on to it.
9. Layer grated cheese on top of it.
10. Bake at 180°C for 25 minutes, until the cheese starts to melt.
11. Serve hot.

Nutrition:

- 504 Calories
- 29g Fat
- 44g Protein

Pumpkin Chocolate Cheesecake

Difficulty: Difficult
Preparation Time: 10 minutes
Cooking Time: 40 minutes
Servings: 2
Ingredients:

- Optavia Essential Decadent Double Chocolate Brownie – 4 sachets (2 healthy fat)
- Butter, unsalted, melted – 1 tbsp (1/2 healthy fat)
- Coldwater – 4 tbsp (1 condiment)
- Greek yogurt, plain, low fat – 2 cups (1/2 healthy fat)
- Cream cheese, light, softened – 5 tbsp (2 healthy fat)
- Pumpkin puree – 6 tbsp (3 lean)
- Egg – 2 (1 healthy fat)
- Stevia – 4 packets (1/4 condiment)
- Vanilla extract – 1 tsp (1/2 condiment)
- Pumpkin pie spice – 1 tsp (1/2 condiment)
- Salt – 1/8 tsp (1/4 condiment)

Directions:

1. Mix the Decadent Double Chocolate Brownie, water, and butter in a medium bowl thoroughly.

2. Preheat the air fryer to 175°C.

3. Grease 4 air fry oven-safe springform pan and evenly place the chocolate brownie mixture.

4. Push the mixture firmly to the bottom of the pan to form a thin crust.

5. Bake it for 15 minutes.

6. Now combine the rest of the ingredients in a medium-size bowl until they become a smooth paste.

7. Transfer it evenly to the springform pans.

8. Reduce the baking temperature to 150°C and bake it for 30-35 minutes until the center becomes firm and the edges start to brown.

9. Pull it from the air fryer and allow them to settle down the temperature.

10. Serve fresh.

Nutrition:

- 518 Calories
- 28g Fat
- 29g Protein

Air Fried Cauliflower Ranch Chips

Difficulty: Easy

Preparation Time: 5 minutes

Cooking Time: 12 minutes

Servings: 2

Ingredients:

- Raw cauliflower, grated - ½ cup (1/4 green)
- Parsley - ¼ tsp (1/8 green)
- Basil - ¼ tsp (1/8 green)
- Dill - ¼ tsp (1/8 green)
- Chives - ¼ tsp (1/8 green)
- Garlic powder - ¼ tsp (1/8 condiment)
- Onion powder - ¼ tsp (1/8 condiment)
- Pepper, ground - ¼ tsp (1/8 condiment)
- Parmesan cheese - ¼ cup (1/8 healthy fat)
- Cooking spray – as required (1/2 healthy fat)

Directions:

1. Preheat the air fryer to 230°C.

2. Using a medium bowl, mix all the ingredients.

3. Line the air fryer baking tray with parchment paper.

4. Scoop 1 tbsp mixture and place it on the parchment paper without overlapping one another.

5. Bake for 12 minutes by flipping side halfway through.

6. Serve hot.

Nutrition:

- 65 Calories
- 3.6g Fat
- 4g Protein

Air Fryer Mint Cookies

Difficulty: Average

Preparation Time: 5 minutes

Cooking Time: 15 minutes

Servings: 2

Ingredients:

- Optavia Essentials Decadent Double Chocolate Brownie – 2 sachets (1 condiment)
- Optavia Essential Chocolate Mint Cookie Bars (2 healthy fats)
- Almond milk, unsweetened – 2 tbsp (1 healthy fat)
- Egg white – 2 (1/2 healthy fat)

Directions:

1. Preheat the air fryer to 180°C.

2. In a mixer blender, crush the chocolate mint bars.

3. Combine chocolate brownie, crushed chocolate mint bars, almond milk, and egg whites in a large bowl.

4. Evenly transfer the mix to 8 cookies ramekins.

5. Place it in the air fryer grill tray and bake for 15 minutes until the top becomes firm.

6. Allow it to settle down the heat and serve.

Nutrition:

- 187 Calories
- 4.1g Fat
- 5g Protein

Cheesy Broccoli Bites

Difficulty: Average
Preparation Time: 5 minutes
Cooking Time: 40 minutes
Servings: 2
Ingredients:

- Frozen broccoli – 3 cups (2 greens)
- Scallions, thinly sliced - ¼ cup (1/2 green)
- Eggs – 2 (1 healthy fat)
- Cottage cheese – 1 cup (1/2 healthy fat)
- Mozzarella cheese, grated - ¾ cup (1/2 healthy fat)
- Parmesan cheese, shredded - ¼ cup (1/4 healthy fat)
- Olive oil – 1 tsp (1/2 condiment)
- Garlic powder - ½ tsp (1/2 condiment)
- Salt – 1/8 tsp (1/4 condiment)
- Water – 2 cups (1 healthy fat)

Directions:

1. Preheat the air fryer to 190°C.

2. Place the broccoli in an air fryer, save bowl, and pour water.

3. Air fryer it for 10 minutes until the broccoli becomes tender.

4. Drain the water and transfer the broccoli into the blender.

5. Blitz it until it chopped well.

6. Now add cottage cheese, scallions, parmesan, mozzarella, eggs, olive oil, salt, and garlic into the blender.

7. Pulse it until it gets mixed well.

8. Transfer it to 12 muffin tins evenly after greasing them.

9. Place it in the air fryer and bake for 30 minutes until the filling becomes firm and its top turns to a golden brown.

10. After baking, remove them from the air fryer.

11. Allow it to settle down the heat and serve.

Nutrition:

- 366 Calories
- 15.1g Fat
- 41g Protein

Cauliflower & Tomato Egg Muffins Air Fried

Difficulty: Difficult
Preparation Time: 10 minutes
Cooking Time: 25 minutes
Servings: 2
Ingredients:

For Egg Muffin

- Eggs – 4 (2 healthy fats)
- Liquid egg whites – 1 cup (1/2 healthy fat)
- Greek yogurt, plain, low fat - ¼ cup (1/4 healthy fat)
- Salt - ¼ tsp (1/4 condiment)

For Cauliflower, Mozzarella & Tomato Mix

- Cauliflower rice, frozen – 6 oz (3 greens)
- Mozzarella cheese, low fat – 1 oz (1/2 healthy fat)
- Cherry tomatoes – 1 cup (1 green)
- Water – 2 cups (1 condiment)

Directions:

1. Thaw the frozen cauliflower rice for 10 minutes.

2. Preheat the air fryer to 190°C.

3. Cook the cauliflower rice in the air fryer by adding 2 cups of water for 10 minutes.

4. Drain the water using a sieve and keep aside ready.

5. In a large bowl, combine Greek yogurt, egg whites, eggs, cheese, and salt.

6. Add all the vegetables to the bowl mix to combine well.

7. Take 12 muffin tins and lightly spray with cooking oil.

8. Transfer the mixture evenly into the muffin tins.

9. Place them in the air fryer and bake for 25 minutes until the center portion becomes hard.

10. Do a toothpick test by inserting it in the center and check if it comes out clean.

11. Pull it out and allow it to settle down the heat before serving.

12. Enjoy your muffin.

Nutrition:

- 286 Calories
- 9.9g Fat
- 33g Protein

Brownie Pies in Peanut Butter

Difficulty: Average

Preparation Time: 10 minutes

Cooking Time: 20 minutes

Servings: 2

Ingredients:

- Optavia Decadent Double Chocolate Brownie – 2 pkt (1 condiment)
- Baking powder - ¼ tsp (1/4 condiment)
- Liquid egg substitute – 3 tbsp (1 healthy fat)
- Vanilla almond milk, unsweetened, divided – 6 tbsp (2 healthy fats)
- Vegetable oil – 1 tsp (1/4 condiment)
- Peanut butter, powdered - ¼ cup (1/2 healthy fat)

Directions:

1. Preheat the air fryer to 180°C.

2. Mix the Decadent Double Chocolate Brownie mixture, egg substitute, baking powder, oil, half of the milk in a large bowl until it becomes a smooth paste.

3. Take 4 muffin tin and spray cooking oil.

4. Evenly fill ¾ portion of the muffin tin and bake in the air fryer for 20 minutes.

5. When the center becomes firm, insert a toothpick and check whether it comes out clean so that you can confirm the doneness of the muffin.

6. Remove it from the air fryer and allow them to cool down.

7. Now mix the remaining milk and powdered peanut butter in a medium bowl.

8. Slice the muffin horizontally and spread the peanut butter paste onto one half.

9. Situate the other half on top and serve.

Nutrition:

- 281 Calories
- 9.8g Fat
- 7g Protein

Cloud Garlic Bread Breakfast

Difficulty: Difficult

Preparation Time: 10 minutes

Cooking Time: 30 minutes

Servings: 2

Ingredients:

- Eggs, medium (separate yellow and white) – 2 (1 healthy fat)
- Cream cheese, low fat - 1½ tbsp (1 healthy fat)
- Sweetener, no-calorie - ½ pkt (1/2 condiment)
- Tartar cream - ¼ tsp (1/4 condiment)

For Garlic Bread

- Butter, unsalted, melted – 1tsp (1/2 healthy fat)
- Garlic powder – 1/8 tsp (1/4 condiment)
- Italian seasoning - ¼ tsp (1/4 condiment)
- Salt – 1/8 tsp (1/4 condiment)

Directions:

1. Combine thoroughly cream cheese, egg yolks, the sweetener in a medium bowl.

2. Beat egg whites in a large bowl along with tartar cream until the whites become stiff peaks.

3. Now carefully fold the yellow yolk mixture into the egg whites without breaking the whites.

4. Line a parchment paper in the air fryer baking tray and place 4 scoops of the mixture without overlapping one another.

5. Set the temperature to 150°C and bake for 20 minutes.

6. Take out the bread, and brush butter on top and sprinkle the seasoning, garlic powder, and salt.

7. Place it again into the air fryer and bake for further 10 minutes until the top becomes golden brown.

8. After baking, allow it to settle down the heat before serving.

Nutrition:

- 115 Calories
- 8.8g Fat
- 6g Protein

Red Pepper & Kale Egg Muffins Air Fried

Difficulty: Average

Preparation Time: 10 minutes

Cooking Time: 25 minutes

Servings: 2

Ingredients:

For Egg Muffin

- Eggs – 4 (1 healthy fat)
- Liquid egg whites – 1 cup (1/2 healthy fat)
- Greek yogurt, plain, low fat - ¼ cup (1/4 healthy fat)
- Salt - ¼ tsp (1/4 condiment)

For Red Bell Pepper, Goat Cheese & Kale Mix

- Red bell pepper, cored and chopped – 6 oz. (3 greens)
- Kale, frozen, chopped – 5 oz (2 greens)
- Goat cheese – 1 oz (1/2 healthy fat)

Directions:

1. Thaw the frozen cauliflower rice for 10 minutes.

2. Preheat the air fryer to 190°C.

3. In a large bowl, combine Greek yogurt, egg whites, eggs, cheese, and salt.

4. Add all the vegetables to the bowl mix to combine well.

5. Take 12 muffin tins and lightly spray with cooking oil.

6. Transfer the mixture evenly into the muffin tins.

7. Place them in the air fryer and bake for 25 minutes until the center portion becomes hard.

8. Do a toothpick test by inserting it in the center and check if it comes out clean.

9. Take it out from the air fryer and allow it to settle down the heat before serving.

10. Enjoy your muffin.

Nutrition:

- 323 Calories
- 15.4g Fat
- 34g Protein

Lemon Garlic Oregano Boneless Chicken

Difficulty: Average

Preparation Time: 5 minutes

Cooking Time: 44 minutes

Servings: 2

Ingredients:

- Chicken breast boneless, skinless - ½ lb. (1 lean)
- Lemon juice – 1 tbsp (1/2 condiment)
- Clove Garlic, minced – 1 (1/2 condiment)
- Oregano fresh, minced – 1 tbsp (1/2 green)
- Black pepper, ground - ¼ tsp (1/4 condiment)
- Salt - ¼ tsp (1/4 condiment)
- Asparagus ends trimmed – 1 lb. (2 greens)
- Water – 1 cup (1/2 condiment)

Directions:

1. Soak, wash, and pat dry chicken.

2. Situate the chicken in a big bowl and marinate with pepper, lemon juice, salt, garlic, and oregano.

3. Place the marinated chicken in the air fry grill tray.

4. Broil at 175°C for 40 minutes until the meat's internal temperature reaches 70°C.

5. After broiling, remove it from the air fryer and set it aside.

6. Now place the asparagus in the air fry ray and pour 1 cup water.

7. Air fry at 175°C for 4 minutes until the asparagus becomes tender.

8. Remove it from the air fryer and drain the water.

9. Slice the chicken and serve along with asparagus.

Nutrition:

- 258 Calories
- 11g Fat
- 29g Protein

Chicken Continental Salad

Difficulty: Easy
Preparation Time: 15 minutes
Cooking Time: 40 minutes
Servings: 2
Ingredients:
Salad making:

- Eggplant, chopped - ½ cup. (1/2 green)
- Zucchini, chopped - ½ cup. (1/2 green)
- Cherry tomatoes halved - ½ cup. (1/2 green)
- Romaine lettuce – 3 cups (2 greens)
- Parmesan cheese, shredded - ¼ cup (1/4 healthy fat)
- Chicken breast - ¾ lb. (1 lean)
- Salt - ¼ tsp (1/4 condiment)
- Pepper ground - ¼ tsp (1/4 condiment)

Dressing:

- Fresh lemon juice - ½ tsp (1/2 condiment)
- Dijon mustard - ¼ tsp (1/4 condiment)
- Worcestershire sauce - ½ tsp (1/4 condiment)
- Clove garlic – 1 (1/4 condiment)
- Salt - ½ tsp (1/4 condiment)
- Pepper ground - ¼ tsp (1/4 condiment)
- Parmesan cheese, shredded – 1 tbsp (1/2 healthy fat)
- Mayonnaise, light – 1 tbsp (1/2 healthy fat)
- Olive oil, extra virgin - 1½ tsp (1 condiment)

Directions:

- Preheat the air fryer to 200°C.
- Clean, wash, and drain the chicken breast.
- Rub salt, pepper on the chicken breast, and keep aside for 15 minutes for marinating.
- Line a baking paper in the air fryer tray and spray some cooking on to it.
- Place zucchini and eggplant on the baking paper.

- Start baking by shaking intermittently for 20 minutes until they become tender.
- For preparing the dressing, combine all the ingredients in the dressing section in a medium bowl.
- Put the tomatoes, lettuce, air fried veggies in the dressing mixture, and toss well.
- Place the marinated chicken on the air fryer grill tray and broil for 20 minutes until the inside meat temperature reaches 75°C.
- After cooking, remove it and allow it to cool down.
- Slice the chicken and serve along with the dressing.

Nutrition:

- 370 Calories
- 14.3g Fat
- 45g Protein

Asparagus Risotto with Chicken

Difficulty: Difficult
Preparation Time: 20 minutes
Cooking Time: 38 minutes
Servings: 2
Ingredients:

- Chicken breast – 1 lb. (2 lean)
- Pepper ground - ½ tsp (1/4 condiment)
- Salt - ¼ tsp (1/4 condiment)
- Butter, melted – 1 tbsp (1/2 healthy fat)
- Cauliflower, finely grated - ¾ lb. (1 green)
- Asparagus, finely chopped - ¼ lb. (1/2 green)
- Chicken stock - ¼ cup (1/2 condiment)
- Nutritional yeast flakes – 2 tbsp (1 condiment)

Directions:

1. Soak the chicken in running water and pat dry.
2. Preheat the air fryer to 180°C.
3. Season the chicken with pepper and salt.
4. Place it in an air fryer safe casserole and pour melted butter over it.
5. Air fry it for 30 minutes until the internal temperature of the meat reaches 70°C.
6. Pull it out from the air fryer and let it cool.

7. Now place the asparagus and cauliflower rice in the air fryer tray.

8. Pour the chicken stock over it and air fry for 8 minutes until the veggies become tender.

9. After cooking, remove the risotto and mix the yeast.

10. Cut the chicken and serve along with the risotto.

Nutrition:

- 382 Calories
- 8.6g Fat
- 60g Protein

Portabella Mushrooms Stuffed with Cheese

Difficulty: Difficult

Preparation Time: 15 minutes

Cooking Time: 17 minutes

Servings: 2

Ingredients:

- Portabella mushroom caps, large – 4 (2 leans)
- Soy sauce – 1 tbsp (1/2 condiment)
- Lemon juice – 1 tbsp (1/2 condiment)
- Olive oil, divided – 1 tsp (1/4 condiment)
- Mozzarella cheese, low fat, grated – 2 cups (1 healthy fat)
- Tomato, fresh, diced - ½ cup (1/2 green)
- Clove Garlic, finely grated – 1 clove (1/4 green)
- Cilantro, fresh, chopped – 1 tbsp (1/4 green)

Directions:

1. Make bowls by scooping the flesh from the interior of the mushroom caps.

2. Set the air fryer temperature to 200°C and preheat.

3. Mix the soy sauce, lemon juice, and half a portion of olive oil in a small bowl.

4. Marinate the mixture on the mushroom cap both inside and outside.

5. Line foil coated baking paper in the air fryer tray.

6. Place the marinated mushroom cap in the tray and bake for 10 minutes until they become tender.

7. Now combine tomatoes, mozzarella, garlic, remaining olive oil, and Italian seasoning in a medium bowl.

8. Fill the mushroom caps with the mixture evenly.

9. Bake it in the air fryer for 7 minutes, until the cheese starts to melt.

10. Sprinkle cilantro on top and serve.

Nutrition:

- 250 Calories
- 4.4g Fat
- 40g Protein

Cloud Focaccia Bread Breakfast

Difficulty: Difficult

Preparation Time: 10 minutes

Cooking Time: 30 minutes

Servings: 2

Ingredients:

- Eggs, medium (separate yellow and white) – 2 (1 healthy fat)
- Cream cheese, low fat - 1½ tbsp (1 healthy fat)
- Sweetener, no-calorie - ½ pkt (1/2 condiment)
- Tartar cream - ¼ tsp (1/4 condiment)

For Focaccia Bread

- Olive oil – ½ tsp
- Rosemary - ½ tsp (1/2 green)
- Salt – 1/8 tsp (1/4 condiment)

Directions:

1. Combine thoroughly cream cheese, egg yolks, the sweetener in a medium bowl.

2. Beat egg whites in a large bowl along with tartar cream until the whites become stiff peaks.

3. Now carefully fold the yellow yolk mixture into the egg whites without breaking the whites.

4. Line a parchment paper in the air fryer baking tray and place 4 scoops of the mixture without overlapping one another.

5. Set the temperature to 150°C and bake for 20 minutes.

6. Take out the bread, and brush olive oil on top and sprinkle Rosemary and salt.

7. Place it again into the air fryer and bake for further 10 minutes until the top becomes golden brown.

8. After baking, allow it to settle down the heat before serving.

Nutrition:

- 90 Calories
- 6.5g Fat
- 6g Protein

Breakfast Scones with Blueberry Almond

Difficulty: Difficult

Preparation Time: 10 minutes

Cooking Time: 20 minutes

Servings: 2

Ingredients:

- Optavia Blueberry Almond Hot Cereal – 2 sachets (1/2 healthy fat)
- Flaxseed ground - ¼ cup (1/4 condiment)
- Sugar substitute, zero-calorie – 1 pkt (1/4 condiment)
- Baking powder - ½ tsp (1/4 condiment)
- Solid butter, unsalted, cut into ½" thickness – 1 tbsp. (1/2 healthy fat)
- Liquid egg white - 1½ tbsp (1 healthy fat)
- Greek yogurt, plain, low fat - 1½ tbsp (1 lean)
- Cinnamon ground – 1/8 tsp (1/4 condiment)

Directions:

1. Combine Blueberry Almond Hot Cereal, baking powder, and sugar substitute in a food processor.

2. Put butter cubes and blitz to form a rough, coarse meal. Let there be rice-sized butter pieces to get the scone structure.

3. Now add Greek yogurt, egg white, almond extract, cashew milk, and process until it turns to a dough form.

4. Line a baking paper in the air fryer baking tray.

5. Make 4 flat circles of dough and place them on the baking paper.

6. Drizzle some cinnamon powder on top.

7. Bake it at 205°C for 20 minutes, until it turns to a golden brown.

8. Allow it to cool and cut into half to make 8 wedges.

9. Serve and enjoy.

Nutrition:

- 277 Calories
- 13.6g Fat
- 7g Protein

Meat Recipes

Air Fried Philly Cheesesteak Taquitos

Difficulty: Average

Preparation Time: 20 minutes

Cooking Time: 6-8 hours

Servings: 6

Ingredients

- Dry Italian dressing mix: one package (1 condiment)
- Super Soft Corn Tortillas: one pack (1 healthy fat)
- Green peppers: two pieces, chopped (1/2 green)
- 12 cups of lean beef steak strips (3 leans)
- Beef stock: 2 cups (1 condiment)
- Lettuce shredded, one cup (1/2 green)
- Provolone cheese: ten slices (1 healthy fat)

Direction

1. In a slow cooker, add onion, beef, broth, pepper and seasonings.
2. Cover then cook at low heat for 6 or 8 hours.
3. Heat the tortillas for two minutes in the microwave.
4. Allow the air fryer to preheat to 350F.
5. Remove the cheesesteak from the slow cooker, add 2-3 tablespoons of steak to the tortilla.
6. Add some cheese, roll the tortilla well, and place in a deep fryer basket.
7. Make all the tortillas you want.
8. Lightly brush with olive oil
9. Cook for 6-8 minutes.
10. Flip the tortillas over and brush more oil as needed.
11. Serve with chopped lettuce and enjoy

Nutrition

- 220 calories
- 21g protein
- 16g fat

Air Fryer Pork Taquitos

Difficulty: Average

Preparation Time: 10 minutes

Cooking Time: 20 minutes

Servings: 10

Ingredients

- Pork tenderloin: 3 cups, cooked & shredded (2 leans)
- Shredded mozzarella: 2 and 1/2 cups, fat-free (1 healthy fat)
- 10 small tortillas (1 healthy fat)
- Salsa for dipping (1 condiment)
- 1 juice of a lime (1/4 condiment)

Direction

1. Allow the air fryer to preheat to 380 F.
2. Add the lime juice to the pork and mix well
3. With a damp towel over the tortilla, microwave for ten seconds to soften it
4. Add the pork filling and cheese on top, in a tortilla, roll the tortilla tightly.
5. Situate the tortillas on a greased baking sheet
6. Sprinkle oil on the tortillas. Bake for 7-10 minutes or until the tortillas are golden, turn them halfway.
7. Serve with salad.

Nutrition

- 253 Calories
- 18g Fat
- 20g Protein

Roasted Garlic Bacon and Potatoes

Difficulty: Easy

Preparation Time: 5 minutes

Cooking Time: 25 minutes

Servings: 4

Ingredients:

- 4 medium-sized potatoes (1 healthy fat)
- 4 strips of streaky bacon (1 lean)
- 2 sprigs of rosemary (1 green)

- 6 cloves of garlic, smashed, unpeeled (1/2 condiment)

- 3 tsp of vegetable oil (1/2 condiment)

Directions:

1. Preheat Air fryer to 390°F.

2. Put the smashed garlic, bacon, potatoes, rosemary, and then the oil in a bowl. Stir thoroughly.

3. Place into air fryer basket and roast until golden for about 25 minutes.

Nutrition:

- 114 Calories

- 8.1g Fat

- 6.2g Protein

Low Carb Pork Dumplings with Dipping Sauce

Difficulty: Difficult

Preparation Time: 30 minutes

Cooking Time: 20 minutes

Servings: 6

Ingredients

- 18 dumpling wrappers (1 healthy fat)

- One teaspoon olive oil (1/4 condiment)

- Bok choy: 4 cups(chopped) (2 leans)

- Rice vinegar: 2 tablespoons (1/2 condiment)

- Diced ginger: 1 tablespoon (1/4 condiment)

- Crushed red pepper: 1/4 teaspoon (1/2 green)

- Diced garlic: 1 tablespoon (1/2 condiment)

- Lean ground pork: 1/2 cup (2 leans)

- Lite soy sauce: 2 teaspoons (1/2 condiment)

- Honey: 1/2 tsp. (1/4 healthy fat)

- Toasted sesame oil: 1 teaspoon (1/4 condiment)

- Finely chopped scallions (1 green)

Directions

1. In a large skillet, heat the olive oil, add the bok choy, cook for 6 minutes and add the garlic, ginger and cook for one minute. Transfer this mixture to a paper towel and pat dry any excess oil

2. In a bowl, add the mixture of bok choy, chopped chili and lean ground pork and mix well.

3. Place gnocchi wrap on a plate and add a spoon to fill half of the wrapper. With water, seal the edges and fold them.

4. Spray air fryer basket with air, add dumplings into air fryer basket, and cook at 375 F for 12 minutes or until golden brown.

5. Meanwhile, to make the sauce, combine the sesame oil, rice vinegar, shallot, soy sauce and honey in a mixing bowl.

6. Serve the gnocchi with the sauce.

Nutrition:

- 140 Calories

- 5g Fat

- 12g Protein

Chinese Pancetta Lunch Mix

Difficulty: Average

Preparation Time: 10 minutes

Cooking Time: 12 minutes

Servings: 4

Ingredients:

- 2 eggs (1 healthy fat)

- 2 pounds Pancetta, cut into medium cubes (1 lean)

- 1 cup cornstarch (1/2 condiment)

- 1 tsp. sesame oil (1/2 condiment)

- Salt and black pepper to the taste (1/2 condiment)

- A pinch of Chinese five-spice (1/2 condiment)

- 3 tbsp. canola oil (1/2 healthy fat)

- Sweet ketchup for serving (1/2 condiment)

Directions:

1. In a bowl, mix five spices with salt, pepper, and cornstarch and mix.

2. Scourge eggs with the sesame oil and beat well.

3. Dip the bacon cubes into the cornstarch mixture, then dip the eggs and place them in the air fryer you greased with canola oil.

4. Bake at 340 ° F for 12 minutes, shaking the fryer once.

5. Serve the bacon for lunch with the sweet ketchup on the side.

Nutrition:

- 125 Calories
- 7.9g Fat
- 8.3g Protein

Pancetta Chops with Pineapple-Jalapeno Salsa

Difficulty: Average

Preparation Time: 20 minutes

Cooking Time: 20 minutes

Servings: 3

Ingredients

- 3 pieces of Pancetta Chops (roughly 10 ounces each) (1 lean)
- 2 tablespoons parsley (1/2 green)
- 1 tablespoon of ground Coriander (1/4 condiment)
- ¾ cup of olive oil (1/4 condiment)
- 1 tablespoon of finely chopped rosemary (1/4 green)
- 4 ounces of tomatoes, diced (1/4 green)
- 2 cloves of garlic, chopped (1/4 condiment)
- 4 ounces of pineapple, diced (1/2 healthy fat)
- 8 Jalapenos (1/2 green)
- 3 tsps. of Dijon Mustard (1/4 condiment)
- 1½ tsp. of sugar (1/8 condiment)
- 4 ounces of lemon juice (1/8 condiment)
- 3 tbsp. of finely chopped Cilantro (1/2 green)
- 2½ tsp. of salt (1/8 condiment)

Direction

1. Place the rosemary, sugar, mustard, coriander, ¼ cup of olive oil, 1 tablespoon of coriander, 1 ½ teaspoons of salt and 1 tablespoon of parsley in a mixing bowl and mix thoroughly. Add the bacon cutlets and mix.

2. Fill in marinade into a resealable plastic bag and refrigerate for about 3 hours.

3. Heat your deep fryer to 390 ° F.

4. Place the jalapenos in a bowl and season with 1 tsp. of oil to cover them evenly. Transfer the jalapenos to the air fryer and cook for about

7 minutes. Remove from the deep fryer and set aside to cool.

5. Once cooled, peel, remove the seeds and chop the jalapenos into small pieces and transfer them to a bowl. Add the pineapple, tomatoes, garlic and lemon juice, the rest of the oil, parsley, coriander and salt. Stir and set the sauce aside.

6. Remove the bacon chops from the refrigerator and allow to rest for 30 minutes at room temperature before cooking.

7. Place the ribs in the air fryer and roast at 390 ° F for about 12 minutes. The bacon cutlets are well cooked when the internal temperature is 140 ° F.

Nutrition

- 104 Calories
- 8.7g Fat
- 6.7g Protein

Beef Lunch Meatballs

Difficulty: Easy

Preparation Time: 10 minutes

Cooking Time: 15 minutes

Servings: 4

Ingredients:

- ½ pound beef, ground (1/2 lean)
- ½ pound Italian sausage, chopped (1/2 lean)
- ½ tsp. garlic powder (1/4 condiment)
- ½ tsp. onion powder (1/4 condiment)
- Salt and black pepper to the taste (1/4 condiment)
- ½ cup cheddar cheese, grated (1/2 healthy fat)
- Mashed potatoes for serving (1/2 healthy fat)

Directions:

1. In a bowl, mix the beef with the sausage, garlic powder, onion powder, salt, pepper and cheese, mix well and form 16 meatballs with this mixture.

2. Situate the meatballs in your air fryer and cook them at 370 ° F for 15 minutes.

3. Serve the meatballs with some mashed potatoes on the side.

Nutrition:

- 132 Calories
- 6.7g Fat
- 5.5g Protein

Air Fryer Whole Wheat Crusted Pork Chops

Difficulty: Average
Preparation Time: 10 minutes
Cooking Time: 12 minutes
Servings: 4
Ingredients

- Whole-wheat breadcrumbs: 1 cup (1/2 healthy fat)
- Salt: ¼ teaspoon (1/4 condiment)
- Pork chops: 2-4 pieces (center cut and boneless) (2 leans)
- Chili powder: half teaspoon (1/4 condiment)
- Parmesan cheese: 1 tablespoon (1/4 healthy fat)
- Paprika: 1½ teaspoons (1/2 condiment)
- One egg beaten (1 healthy fat)
- Onion powder: half teaspoon (1/4 condiment)
- Granulated garlic: half teaspoon (1/4 condiment)

Direction

1. Allow the air fryer to preheat to 400 F.

2. rub kosher salt on each side of the pork chops, let it rest

3. Add the beaten egg to a large bowl

4. Add the parmesan, breadcrumbs, garlic, pepper, paprika, chili powder and onion powder to a bowl and mix well

5. Dip the pork chop in the egg and then in the breadcrumbs

6. Put it in the air fryer and spray it with oil.

7. Leave to cook for 12 minutes at 400 F. Turn it upside down halfway through cooking. Cook for another six minutes.

8. Serve with salad.

Nutrition

- 425 calories
- 20g fat
- 31g protein

Mustard Glazed Air Fryer Pork Tenderloin

Difficulty: Average
Preparation Time: 10 minutes
Cooking Time: 18 minutes
Servings: 4
Ingredients

- Yellow mustard: ¼ cup (1/2 green)
- One pork tenderloin (1 lean)
- Salt: ¼ tsp (1/4 condiment)
- Honey: 3 Tbsp. (1/2 healthy fat)
- black pepper: 1/8 tsp (1/4 condiment)
- Minced garlic: 1 Tbsp. (1/4 condiment)
- Dried rosemary: 1 tsp (1/4 green)
- Italian seasoning: 1 tsp (1/8 condiment)

Direction

1. Using a knife, cut the top of the pork tenderloin. Add the garlic (minced) into the cuts. Then sprinkle with kosher salt and pepper.

2. In a bowl, add the honey, mustard, rosemary, and Italian seasoning mixture until well blended. Rub this mustard mix all over the pork.

3. Leave to marinate in the refrigerator for at least two hours.

4. Place the pork tenderloin in the basket of the air fryer. Cook for 18-20 minutes at 400 F. With an instant read thermometer, verify that the internal temperature of the pig should be 145 F.

5. Remove from air fryer and serve with a side of salad.

Nutrition

- 390 Calories
- 59g Protein
- 11g Fat

Air Fried Jamaican Jerk Pork

Difficulty: Difficult
Preparation Time: 10 minutes
Cooking Time: 20 minutes
Servings: 4
Ingredients

- Pork, cut into three-inch pieces (1 lean)
- Jerk paste: ¼ cup (1/4 condiment)

Direction

1. Rub the jerk dough on all the pork pieces.

2. Chill to marinate for 4 hours in the refrigerator.

3. Allow the air fryer to preheat to 390 F. Spray with olive oil

4. Before placing it in the air fryer, allow the meat to rest for 20 minutes at room temperature.

5. Cook for 20 minutes at 390 ° F in the air fryer, turn halfway.

6. Remove from air fryer and let sit for ten minutes before slicing.

7. Serve with microgreens.

Nutrition

- 234 Calories
- 31g Protein
- 9g Fat

Steaks and Cabbage

Difficulty: Easy

Preparation Time: 10 minutes

Cooking Time: 10 minutes

Servings: 4

Ingredients:

- ½ pound sirloin steak, cut into strips (1 lean)
- 2 tsp. cornstarch (1/8 condiment)
- 1 tablespoon peanut oil (1/8 condiment)
- 2 cups green cabbage, chopped (1 green)
- 1 yellow bell pepper (1/2 green)
- 2 garlic cloves, minced (1/8 condiment)
- Salt and black pepper to the taste (1/8 condiment)

Directions:

1. In a bowl, mix the cabbage with salt, pepper and peanut oil, mix, transfer to air fryer basket, cook at 370 ° F for 4 minutes and transfer to the bowl.

2. Add the steak strips to the air fryer, also add bell pepper, garlic, salt and pepper, stir and cook for 5 minutes.

3. Add the cabbage on top, mix, divide into plates and serve for lunch. To enjoy!

Nutrition

- 111 Calories
- 7.2g Fat
- 8.7g Protein

Air Fried Masala Chops

Difficulty: Easy

Preparation Time: 9 minutes

Cooking Time: 30 minutes

Servings: 1

Ingredients:

- ½ pound lamb chop, trimmed from fat (1 lean)
- 2 tablespoon ginger paste (1/4 condiment)
- ½ tablespoon red chili powder (1/4 condiment)
- 1 tablespoon garam masala (1/4 condiment)
- ½ teaspoon salt (1/4 condiment)

Directions:

1. Preheat the air fryer to 350F for five minutes.

2. Seal the bottom of the air fryer with foil.

3. Season the lamb chops with the spices.

4. Place inside the air fryer and cook for 25 to 30 minutes

Nutrition:

- 343 Calories
- 46g Protein
- 15g Fat

Stuffed Meatballs

Difficulty: Average

Preparation Time: 10 minutes

Cooking Time: 10 minutes

Servings: 4

Ingredients:

- 1/3 cup bread crumbs (1 healthy fat)
- 3 tbsp. milk (1/2 condiment)
- 1 tablespoon ketchup (1/4 condiment)
- 1 egg (1 healthy fat)
- ½ tsp. marjoram, dried (1/4 condiment)
- Salt and black pepper to the taste (1/8 condiment)
- 1-pound lean beef, ground (1 lean)

- 20 cheddar cheese cubes (1/2 healthy fat)
- 1 tablespoon olive oil (1/8 condiment)

Direction

1. In a bowl, mix the breadcrumbs with ketchup, milk, marjoram, salt, pepper and egg and beat well.

2. Add the beef, mix and form 20 meatballs with this mixture.

3. Shape each meatball around a cube of cheese, sprinkle with oil and rub.

4. Place all the meatballs in your preheated air fryer and cook at 390 ° F for 10 minutes.

5. Serve them for lunch with a side of salad.

Nutrition

- 112 Calories
- 8.2g Fat
- 7.7g Protein

Bacon and Garlic Pizzas

Difficulty: Easy

Preparation Time: 10 minutes

Cooking Time: 10 minutes

Servings: 4

Ingredients:

- 4 dinner rolls, frozen
- 4 garlic cloves minced
- ½ tsp. oregano dried
- ½ tsp. garlic powder
- 1 cup ketchup
- 8 bacon slices, cooked and chopped
- 1 and ¼ cups cheddar cheese, grated

Directions:

1. Place the rolls on a work surface and press them to obtain 4 ovals.

2. Spray each oval with cooking spray, transfer them to the air fryer and cook at 370 ° F for 2 minutes.

3. Spread the ketchup on each oval, divide the garlic, sprinkle with oregano and garlic powder and garnish with bacon and cheese.

4. Return the pizzas to your hot air fryer and cook them at 370 ° F for another 8 minutes.

5. Serve hot for lunch.

Nutrition

- 104 Calories
- 9g Fat
- 8.5g Protein

Air Fried Rib Eye Steak

Difficulty: Average

Preparation Time: 18 minutes

Cooking Time: 15 minutes

Servings: 1

Ingredients:

- ½ pound red eye steak, fat-trimmed
- ½ teaspoon salt
- ¾ teaspoon ground pepper
- ½ teaspoon garlic powder
- ¾ teaspoon steak seasoning

Directions:

1. Preheat the air fryer to 350F for five minutes.

2. Season the steak with the spices.

3. Situate in the air fryer and cook for 15 minutes.

4. Allow to rest before serving.

Nutrition:

- 540 Calories
- 44g Protein
- 28g Fat

Teriyaki Glazed Halibut Steak

Difficulty: Average

Preparation Time: 30 minutes

Cooking Time: 10-15 minutes

Servings: 3

Ingredients

- 1-pound halibut steak (1 lean)

For the Marinade:

- 3 oz. soy sauce, low sodium (1/4 condiment)
- ½ cup mirin (1/4 condiment)
- 2 tbsp. lime juice (1/8 condiment)
- ¼ cup sugar (1/8 condiment)
- ¼ cup orange juice (1/8 condiment)
- ¼ tsp. ginger ground (1/8 condiment)
- ¼ tsp. crushed red pepper flakes (1/8 condiment)

- 1 each garlic clove (smashed) (1/8 condiment)

Direction

1. Place all ingredients for the teriyaki glaze/marinade in a saucepan. Bring to a boil and reduce by half, then allow to cool.

2. When it cools, pour half of the icing/marinade into a zip-up bag along with the halibut, then refrigerate for 30 minutes.

3. Preheat Air fryer to 390 ° F. Place marinated halibut in the Air fryer and cook 10-12 minutes. Rub some of the remaining glaze on the halibut steak.

4. Spread on white rice with basil/mint chutney.

Nutrition

- 116 Calories
- 7g Fat
- 7.2g Protein

Roast Lamb Rack

Difficulty: Difficult

Preparation Time: 12 minutes

Cooking Time: 30 minutes

Servings: 3

Ingredients:

- 1 ½ pounds rack of lamb (1 lean)
- Salt and pepper to taste (1/4 condiment)
- 1 teaspoon grated garlic (1/8 condiment)
- 1 teaspoon cumin seeds (1/4 healthy fat)
- 1 teaspoon olive oil (1/8 condiment)

Directions:

1. Preheat the air fryer to 350F for five minutes.

2. Coat the bottom of the air fryer with foil.

3. Season the rack of lamb with the spices.

4. Place in the air fryer and cook for 25 to 30 minutes.

Nutrition:

- 386 Calories
- 47.3g Protein
- 12g Fat

Air Fryer Pork Chop & Broccoli

Difficulty: Average

Preparation Time: 20 minutes

Cooking Time: 20 minutes

Servings: 2

Ingredients

- Broccoli florets: 2 cups (1 green)
- Bone-in pork chop: 2 pieces (1 lean)
- Paprika: 1/2 tsp. (1/4 condiment)
- Avocado oil: 2 tbsp. (1 healthy fat)
- Garlic powder: 1/2 tsp. (1/4 condiment)
- Onion powder: 1/2 tsp. (1/4 condiment)
- Two cloves of crushed garlic (1/4 condiment)
- Salt: 1 teaspoon divided (1/4 condiment)

Direction

1. Let the air fryer preheat to 350 degrees. Spray the basket with cooking oil

2. Add a spoon. Oil, onion powder, half a teaspoon. of salt, garlic powder and paprika in a bowl mix well, rub this spice mixture on the sides of the pork chop

3. Add the pork chops to the fryer basket and cook for five minutes

4. Meanwhile, add a teaspoon. oil, garlic, half a teaspoon of salt and broccoli in a bowl and coat them well

5. Turn the pork chop and add the broccoli, let it cook for another five minutes.

6. Remove from air fryer and serve.

Nutrition

- 483 Calories
- 20g Fat
- 23g Protein

Air Fryer Steak Bites and Mushrooms

Difficulty: Average

Preparation Time: 9 minutes

Cooking Time: 25 minutes

Servings: 4

Ingredients:

- 1 pound 99% lean steak (fat trimmed), cut into cubes (1 lean)
- 8 ounces mushrooms, sliced (1 healthy fat)
- 1 teaspoon melted butter (1/4 healthy fat)
- ½ teaspoon garlic powder (1/8 condiment)

- Salt and pepper to taste (1/8 condiment)

Directions:

1. Preheat the air fryer to 350F for five minutes.

2. Prep the bottom of the air fryer with foil.

3. Place all ingredients in a bowl. Toss to coat the beef and mushrooms with the seasoning.

4. Place the seasoned beef and mushrooms inside the foil-lined fryer basket.

5. Cook for 20 to 25 minutes.

6. Halfway through the cooking time, open the fryer basket and give a good shake for even cooking.

Nutrition:

- 299 Calories
- 14g Protein
- 5g Fat

Air Fryer Pork Chops

Difficulty: Average
Preparation Time: 6 minutes
Cooking Time: 25 minutes
Servings: 4
Ingredients:

- 1 tablespoon paprika (1/8 condiment)
- 1 ½ teaspoon salt (1/4 condiment)
- 1 teaspoon ground mustard (1/8 condiment)
- ¼ teaspoon garlic powder (1/8 condiment)
- 4 center cut bone-in pork chops, trimmed from fat (2 lean)

Directions:

1. Preheat the air fryer to 350F for five minutes.

2. Seal the bottom of the air fryer with foil.

3. Mix together the paprika, salt, mustard, and garlic powder to create a spice rub.

4. Massage the pork chops with the spice rub.

5. Place the seasoned pork chops inside the air fryer and cook for 20 to 25 minutes.

Nutrition:

- 234 Calories
- 40g Protein
- 7g Fat

Air Fryer Meat Loaf

Difficulty: Easy
Preparation Time: 11 minutes
Cooking Time: 20 minutes
Servings: 4
Ingredients:

- 1 pound 99% lean ground beef (1 lean)
- ½ teaspoon garlic powder (1/4 condiment)
- 3 egg whites, beaten (1 healthy fat)
- 1 cup grated kohlrabi (1 healthy fat)
- Salt and pepper to taste (1/4 condiment)

Directions:

1. Preheat the air fryer to 350F for five minutes.

2. In a bowl, mix all ingredients until well combined.

3. Pour the mixture into a greased loaf pan that will fit inside the air fryer. Cover with aluminum foil on top.

4. Place inside the preheated air fryer and cook for 35 to 45 minutes until the meat is cooked through.

5. Allow the meatloaf to cool before slicing.

Nutrition:

- 270 Calories
- 34g Protein
- 10g Fat

Air Fried Riblets

Difficulty: Easy
Preparation Time: 9 minutes
Cooking Time: 25 minutes
Servings: 2
Ingredients:

- 1-pound pork riblets (1 lean)
- 1 teaspoon salt (1/8 condiment)
- 6 cloves of garlic, minced (1/4 condiment)

Directions:

1. Preheat the air fryer to 350F for five minutes.

2. Wrap the bottom of the air fryer with foil.

3. Season the pork riblets with salt and garlic.

4. Place inside the air fryer and cook for 20 to 25 minutes.

Nutrition:

- 288 Calories
- 39g Protein
- 12g Fat

Rosemary Crusted Lamb Chops

Difficulty: Difficult

Preparation Time: 13 minutes

Cooking Time: 25 minutes

Servings: 2

Ingredients:

- 1-pound lamb chops, trimmed of fat (1 lean)
- 2 tablespoons fresh rosemary (1/4 green)
- ½ teaspoon salt (1/8 condiment)
- 1 teaspoon ground black pepper (1/8 condiment)
- 3 cloves garlic, minced (1/4 condiment)

Directions:

1. Preheat the air fryer to 350F for five minutes.
2. Seal the bottom of the air fryer with foil.
3. Season the lamb chops with the spices and condiments.
4. Place inside the air fryer basket.
5. Cook for 25 minutes until golden.

Nutrition:

- 335 Calories
- 45g Protein
- 15.7g Fat

Air Fried Beef Jerky

Difficulty: Easy

Preparation Time: 11 minutes

Cooking Time: 15 minutes

Servings: 2

Ingredients:

- 12 ounces, sirloin beef, sliced (2 lean)
- 1 clove of garlic, minced (1/2 condiment)
- Salt and pepper to taste (1/2 condiment)

Directions:

1. Preheat the air fryer to 350F for five minutes.
2. Line the bottom of the air fryer with foil.

3. Place all ingredients in a bowl and toss to coat the beef slices with the seasoning.
4. Place beef slices in the air fryer and cook for 15 minutes.

Nutrition:

- 333 Calories
- 35g Protein
- 14g Fat

Air Fryer Roasted Beef

Difficulty: Average

Preparation Time: 8 minutes

Cooking Time: 60 minutes

Servings: 8

Ingredients:

- 4 pounds beef roast (1 lean)
- 2 teaspoons garlic powder (1/4 condiment)
- ½ teaspoon salt (1/8 condiment)
- ½ teaspoon pepper (1/8 condiment)
- 2 teaspoons thyme (1/4 green)
- 1 tablespoon olive oil (1/8 condiment)

Directions:

1. Preheat the air fryer to 350F for five minutes.
2. Pat dry the beef and place it on a working surface.
3. In a small bowl, combine the condiments and spices to form a dry rub.
4. Massage the beef with the dry rub all over the beef.
5. Place the seasoned beef inside the preheated air fryer and cook for 60 minutes.
6. Allow the beef to rest before slicing.

Nutrition:

- 434 Calories
- 61g Protein
- 12g Fat

Peppery Roasted Potatoes with Smoked Bacon

Difficulty: Average

Preparation Time: 15 minutes

Cooking Time: 11 minutes

Servings: 2

Ingredients

- 5 small rashers smoked bacon (1 lean)
- 1/3 tsp. garlic powder (1/4 condiment)
- 1 tsp. sea salt (1/4 condiment)
- 2 tsp. paprika (1/4 condiment)
- 1/3 tsp. ground black pepper (1/4 condiment)
- 1 bell pepper (1/2 green)
- 1 tsp. mustard (1/4 condiment)
- 2 habanero peppers, halved (1/2 green)

Direction

1. Simply toss all the ingredients in a mixing dish; then transfer them to your air fryer's basket.
2. Air-fry at 375F for 10 minutes. Serve warm.

Nutrition

- 122 Calories
- 9g Fat
- 10g Protein

Gluten-Free Air Fryer Chicken Fried Brown Rice

Difficulty: Average

Preparation Time: 10 minutes

Cooking Time: 20 minutes

Servings: 2

Ingredients

- Chicken Breast: 1 Cup (1 lean)
- White Onion: 1/4 cup chopped (1/2 green)
- Celery: 1/4 Cup chopped (1/2 green)
- Cooked brown rice: 4 Cups (2 healthy fat)
- Carrots: 1/4 cup chopped (1/2 green)

Directions

1. Place the foil on the air fryer basket, make sure to leave room for airflow, roll up on the sides
2. Spray the film with olive oil. Mix all the ingredients.
3. On top of the foil, add all the ingredients to the air fryer basket.
4. Give a splash of olive oil in the mixture.
5. Cook for five minutes at 390 ° F.
6. Open the air fryer and give the mixture a spin
7. cook for another five minutes at 390 ° F.
8. Remove from air fryer and serve hot.

Nutrition

- 350 Calories
- 6g Fat
- 22g Protein

Air Fried Burger Patties

Difficulty: Easy

Preparation Time: 8 minutes

Cooking Time: 15 minutes

Servings: 4

Ingredients:

- 1 teaspoon liquid smoke (1/8 condiment)
- ½ teaspoon garlic powder (1/8 condiment)
- ½ teaspoon salt (1/8 condiment)
- ½ teaspoon ground black pepper (1/8 condiment)
- 1 pound 99% lean ground beef (1 lean)
- 1 teaspoon parsley (1/2 green)

Directions:

1. Preheat the air fryer to 350F for five minutes.
2. Place all ingredients in a bowl.
3. Mix until well combined.
4. Form four burger patties from the mixture using your hands.
5. Place the patties inside the fridge to firm up.
6. After 2 hours, place the patties inside the air fryer basket.
7. Cook for 15 minutes.

Nutrition:

- 246 Calories
- 31g Protein
- 13g Fat

Pork Tenderloin with Fried Bell Peppers

Difficulty: Average

Preparation Time: 18 minutes

Cooking Time: 20 minutes

Servings: 4

Ingredients:

- 2 large bell peppers, seeded and julienned (1 green)
- 10 ounces Cremini mushrooms, diced (2 healthy fats)
- 1-pound pork tenderloin (1 lean)
- Salt and pepper to taste (1/8 condiment)

Directions:

1. Preheat the air fryer to 350F for five minutes.

2. Line the bottom of the air fryer with foil.

3. Place all ingredients in a bowl and toss to coat everything with the seasonings.

4. Place inside the air fryer basket and cook for 20 minutes.

5. Halfway through the cooking time, give the fryer basket a shake for even cooking.

Nutrition:

- 385 Calories
- 37g Protein
- 4.7g Fat

Cornbread with Pulled Pancetta

Difficulty: Easy

Preparation Time: 24 minutes

Cooking Time: 19 minutes

Servings: 2

Ingredients

- 2½ cups pulled Pancetta (1 lean)
- 1 tsp. dried rosemary (1/4 green)
- 1/2 tsp. chili powder (1/4 condiment)
- 3 cloves garlic (1/4 condiment)
- 1/2 recipe cornbread (1 healthy fat)
- 1/2 tablespoon brown sugar (1/4 condiment)
- 1/3 cup scallions, thinly sliced (1/2 green)
- 1 tsp. sea salt (1/8 condiment)

Direction

1. Preheat a large non-stick pan over medium heat; now cook the shallots together with the garlic and the pulled bacon.

2. Next, add the sugar, chili powder, rosemary and salt. Cook, stirring regularly until thickened.

3. Preheat your air fryer to 335 ° F. Now, coat two mini loaf pans with cooking spray. Add the pulled bacon mixture and spread over the bottom with a spatula.

4. Spread the previously prepared cornbread batter over the spicy pulled bacon mixture.

5. Bake this cornbread in a preheated air fryer until a centered tester is clean, or for 18 minutes.

Nutrition

- 117 Calories
- 9.4g Fat
- 11g Protein

Pork Rind Nachos

Difficulty: Average

Preparation Time: 5 minutes

Cooking Time: 5 minutes

Servings: 2

Ingredients

- 2 tbsp. of pork rinds (1 lean)
- 1/4 cup shredded cooked chicken (1/2 lean)
- 1/2 cup shredded Monterey jack cheese (1/4 healthy fat)
- 1/4 cup sliced pickled jalapeños (1/4 green)
- 1/4 cup guacamole (1/4 healthy fat)
- 1/4 cup full-fat sour cream (1/4 healthy fat)

Direction

1. Place the pork rinds in a 6-inch round pan. Fill with grilled chicken and Monterey jack cheese. Place the pan in the basket with the air fryer.

2. Set the temperature to 370 ° F and set the timer for 5 minutes or until the cheese has melted.

3. Eat immediately with jalapeños, guacamole, and sour cream.

Nutrition

- 295 calories
- 30g protein
- 27g fat

Air Fryer Italian Pork Chops

Difficulty: Difficult

Preparation Time: 9 minutes

Cooking Time: 25 minutes

Servings: 2

Ingredients:

- 2 boneless pork loin chops, trimmed from fat (1 lean)
- ¼ teaspoon salt (1/8 condiment)
- 1 teaspoon Italian herb seasoning (1/8 condiment)

Directions:

1. Preheat the air fryer to 350F for five minutes.
2. Wrap the bottom of the air fryer with foil.
3. Season the pork loin chops with the spices and seasoning.
4. Place inside the air fryer basket and cook for 20 to 25 minutes.

Nutrition:

- 235 Calories
- 41g Protein
- 3g Fat

Air Fried Pot Roast

Difficulty: Average
Preparation Time: 12 minutes
Cooking Time: 60 minutes
Servings: 8
Ingredients:

- 4 pounds beef chuck roast (2 lean)
- Salt and pepper to taste (1/2 condiment)
- 5 cloves garlic, minced (1/2 condiment)
- 1 teaspoon thyme (1/2 green)

Directions:

1. Preheat the air fryer to 350F for five minutes.
2. Line the bottom of the air fryer with foil.
3. Score the beef using a knife.
4. Season the pot roast with the seasoning.
5. Place inside the air fryer basket and cook for 60 minutes.

Nutrition:

- 420 Calories
- 61g Protein
- 16g Fat

Air Fried Roasted Lamb

Difficulty: Difficult
Preparation Time: 14 minutes
Cooking Time: 25 minutes
Servings: 1
Ingredients:

- 10 ounces butterflied lamb leg roast, fat trimmed (2 lean)
- 1 tablespoon olive oil (1/4 condiment)
- 1 teaspoon rosemary (1/4 green)
- 1 teaspoon thyme (1/4 green)
- ¼ teaspoon salt (1/8 condiment)
- ½ teaspoon black pepper (1/8 condiment)

Directions:

1. Preheat the air fryer to 360F for five minutes.
2. Prepare the bottom of the air fryer with foil.
3. Season the lamb leg roast with spices and condiments.
4. Place in the air fryer and cook for 15 to 20 minutes.

Nutrition:

- 181 Calories
- 18g Protein
- 3g Fat

Mustard Pork Chops

Difficulty: Easy
Preparation Time: 11 minutes
Cooking Time: 20 minutes
Servings: 4
Ingredients:

- 4 tablespoons mustard (1/8 condiment)
- 2 tablespoons minced garlic (1/4 condiment)
- ½ teaspoon salt (1/8 condiment)
- 1 teaspoon ground black pepper (1/8 condiment)
- 4 pork chops, trimmed from fat (2 lean)

Directions:

1. Preheat the air fryer to 350F for five minutes.
2. Seal the bottom of the air fryer with foil.

3.   Place the mustard, garlic, salt, and black pepper in a bowl. Mix until well combined.

4.   Massage the pork chops with the spice rub.

5.   Place seasoned pork chops inside the air fryer and cook for 20 minutes.

Nutrition:

- 346 Calories
- 41g Protein
- 17.9g Fat

Air Fryer Pork Tenderloin

Difficulty: Average

Preparation Time: 13 minutes

Cooking Time: 25 minutes

Servings: 4

Ingredients:

- ½ teaspoon black pepper (1/8 condiment)
- ¼ teaspoon garlic powder (1/8 condiment)
- ¼ teaspoon salt (1/8 condiment)
- 2 pounds pork tenderloin, trimmed from excess fat (1 lean)

Directions:

1.   Preheat the air fryer to 350F for five minutes.

2.   Seal the bottom of the air fryer with foil.

3.   Mix together the black pepper, garlic powder, and salt to create a spice rub.

4.   Massage the pork with the spice rub.

5.   Place the seasoned pork tenderloin inside the air fryer and cook for 20 to 25 minutes.

Nutrition:

- 266 Calories
- 59g Protein
- 7g Fat

Air Fryer Cheesy Pork Chops

Difficulty: Average

Preparation Time: 5 minutes

Cooking Time: 8 minutes

Servings: 2

Ingredients

- 4 lean pork chops (2 leans)
- Salt: half tsp. (1/4 condiment)
- Garlic powder: ½ tsp. (1/4 condiment)

- Shredded cheese: 4 tbsp. (1 healthy fat)
- Chopped cilantro (1 green)

Direction

1.   Let the air fryer preheat to 350 degrees.

2.   With garlic, coriander and salt, rub the pork chops. Put the air fryer on. Let it cook for four minutes. Turn them over and then cook for extra two minutes.

3.   Drizzle the cheese on top and cook for another two minutes or until the cheese has melted.

4.   Serve with salad.

Nutrition

- 467 Calories
- 61g Protein
- 22g Fat

Air Fried Lamb Chops

Difficulty: Difficult

Preparation Time: 12 minutes

Cooking Time: 25 minutes

Servings: 2

Ingredients:

- 5 cloves of garlic, sliced (1/8 condiment)
- 1 teaspoon garam masala (1/8 condiment)
- 1 teaspoon ground cinnamon (1/8 condiment)
- ½ teaspoon cayenne powder (1/8 condiment)
- ½ teaspoon salt (1/8 condiment)
- 1-pound lamb chops, fat trimmed (1 lean)

Directions:

1.   Preheat the air fryer to 350F for five minutes.

2.   Prep bottom of the air fryer with foil.

3.   Place the garlic, garam masala, cinnamon, cayenne pepper, and salt. Mix to create the spice rub.

4.   Massage the lamb chops with the spice rub.

5.   Place inside the air fryer basket.

6.   Cook for 20 to 25 minutes.

Nutrition:

- 338 Calories
- 46g Protein
- 12g Fat

Mutton Chops

Difficulty: Average
Preparation Time: 11 minutes
Cooking Time: 25 minutes
Servings: 8
Ingredients:

- 8 mutton chops, trimmed from fat (2 lean)
- 1 tablespoon crushed garlic (1/4 condiment)
- Salt and pepper to taste (1/4 condiment)
- ½ teaspoon cumin (1/4 condiment)

Directions:

1. Preheat the air fryer to 350F for five minutes.
2. Seal the bottom of the air fryer with foil.
3. Season the mutton chops with spices.
4. Place in the air fryer basket and cook for 25 minutes.
5. Cook in batches if necessary.

Nutrition:

- 168 Calories
- 23g Protein
- 8g Fat

Air Fried Mongolian Beef

Difficulty: Average
Preparation Time: 9 minutes
Cooking Time: 20 minutes
Servings: 4
Ingredients:

- 2 cloves garlic, minced (1/4 condiment)
- 1 cup chopped scallions (1/2 green)
- ½ teaspoon minced ginger (1/4 condiment)
- 1 ½ pounds flank steak, thinly sliced (1 lean)
- 1 teaspoon sesame oil (1/4 condiment)
- Salt and pepper to taste (1/4 condiment)

Directions:

1. Preheat the air fryer to 350F for five minutes.
2. Line the bottom of the air fryer with foil.
3. Place all ingredients in a bowl. Toss to coat beef with the condiments.
4. Place inside the air fryer basket.
5. Cook for 15 to 20 minutes.

Nutrition:

- 258 Calories
- 37g Protein
- 9.7g Fat

Poultry Recipes

Air Fryer Cornish Hen

Difficulty: Average
Preparation Time: 8 minutes
Cooking Time: 25 minutes
Servings: 3
Ingredients:

- One Cornish hen (1 lean)
- Salt & black pepper to taste (1/2 condiment)
- Olive oil spray (1/4 condiment)
- Paprika, ¼ tbsp. (1/4 condiment)

Directions:

1. Mix all spices and Rub the spices all over Cornish hen.
2. Coat the air fryer basket with olive oil.
3. Put Cornish hen in an Air fryer.
4. Cook for 25 minutes at 390 F. flip after half time.
5. Serve with a mixed green salad.

Nutrition:

- 300 Calories
- 25g Protein
- 21g Fat

Herb-Marinated Chicken Thighs

Difficulty: Average
Preparation Time: 9 minutes
Cooking Time: 10 minutes
Servings: 4
Ingredients:

- Chicken thighs: 8 skin-on, bone-in (4 lean)
- Lemon juice: 2 Tablespoon (1/8 condiment)
- Garlic powder: 2 teaspoons (1/8 condiment)
- Spike Seasoning: 1 teaspoon. (1/8 condiment)
- Olive oil: 1/4 cup (1/8 condiment)
- Dried basil: 1 teaspoon (1/2 green)
- Dried oregano: ½ teaspoon. (1/2 green)
- Black Pepper: 1/4 tsp. (1/8 condiment)

Directions:

1. In a bowl, add dried oregano, olive oil, lemon juice, dried sage, garlic powder, Spike Seasoning, onion powder, dried basil, black pepper.
2. In a zip lock bag, add the spice blend and the chicken and mix well.
3. Marinate the chicken in the refrigerator for at least six hours or more.
4. Preheat the air fryer to 360F.
5. Put the chicken in the air fryer basket, cook for six-eight minutes, flip the chicken, and cook for six minutes more.
6. Until the internal chicken temperature reaches 165F.
7. Take out from the air fryer and serve with microgreens.

Nutrition:

- 100 Calories
- 9g Fat
- 4g Protein

Air Fryer Chicken & Broccoli

Difficulty: Average
Preparation Time: 11 minutes
Cooking Time: 15 minutes
Servings: 4
Ingredients:

- Olive oil: 2 Tablespoons (1/8 condiment)
- Chicken breast: 4 cups, bone and skinless (cut into cubes) (2 lean)
- Low sodium soy sauce: 1 Tbsp. (1/8 condiment)
- Garlic powder: half teaspoon (1/8 condiment)
- Rice vinegar: 2 teaspoons (1/8 condiment)
- Broccoli: 1-2 cups, cut into florets (1 green)
- Hot sauce: 2 teaspoons (1/8 condiment)
- Fresh minced ginger: 1 Tbsp. (1/8 condiment)
- Sesame seed oil: 1 teaspoon (1/8 condiment)
- Salt & black pepper, to taste (1/8 condiment)

Directions:

1. In a bowl, add chicken breast, onion, and broccoli. Combine them well.

2. In another bowl, add ginger, oil, sesame oil, rice vinegar, hot sauce, garlic powder, and soy sauce mix it well. Then add the broccoli, chicken, and onions to marinade.

3. Coat well the chicken with sauces. Set aside in the refrigerator for 15 minutes

4. Place chicken mix in one even layer in air fryer basket and cook for 16-20 minutes, at 380 F. halfway through, toss the basket gently and cook the chicken evenly

5. Add five minutes more, if required.

6. Add salt and pepper if needed.

7. Serve warm with lemon wedges

Nutrition:
- 191 Calories
- 7g Fat
- 25g Protein

Orange Chicken Wings

Difficulty: Easy
Preparation Time: 19 minutes
Cooking Time: 14 minutes
Servings: 2
Ingredients:
- Honey: 1 tbsp. (1/2 healthy fat)
- Chicken Wings, Six pieces (3 lean)
- One orange zest and juice (1/2 healthy fat)
- Worcestershire Sauce: 1.5 tbsp. (1/4 condiment)
- Black pepper to taste (1/4 condiment)
- Herbs (sage, rosemary, oregano, parsley, basil, thyme, and mint) (1 green)

Directions:

1. Wash and pat dry the chicken wings

2. In a bowl, add chicken wings, pour zest and orange juice

3. Add the rest of the ingredients and rub on chicken wings. Let it marinate for at least half an hour.

4. Let the Air fryer preheat at 180°C

5. In an aluminum foil, wrap the marinated wings and put them in an air fryer and cook for 20 minutes at 180 C

6. After 20 minutes, remove aluminum foil and brush the sauce over the wings and cook for 15 minutes more. Then again, brush the sauce and cook for another ten minutes.

7. Take out from the air fryer and serve with salad greens.

Nutrition:
- 271 Calories
- 29g Proteins
- 15g Fat

Low Carb Parmesan Chicken Meatballs

Difficulty: Easy
Preparation Time: 19 minutes
Cooking Time: 12 minutes
Servings: 20
Ingredients:
- Pork rinds: 1/2 cup, ground (1 lean)
- Ground chicken: 4 cups (2 lean)
- Parmesan cheese: 1/2 cup grated (1/2 healthy fat)
- Kosher salt: 1 tsp. (1/8 condiment)
- Garlic powder: 1 tsp. (1/8 condiment)
- 1 egg beaten (1/2 healthy fat)
- Paprika: 1 tsp. (1/8 condiment)
- Pepper: 1/2 tsp. (1/8 condiment)
- Breading (1/4 condiment)
- Pork rinds: 1/2 cup ground (1/2 healthy fat)

Directions:

1. Let the Air Fryer pre-heat to 400°F.

2. Add cheese, chicken, egg, pepper, half cup of pork rinds, garlic, salt, and paprika in a big mixing ball. Mix well into a dough, make into 1and half-inch balls.

3. Coat the meatballs in pork rinds(ground).

4. Oil sprays the air fry basket and add meatballs in one even layer.

5. Let it cook for 12 minutes at 400°F, flipping once halfway through.

6. Serve with salad greens.

Nutrition
- 240 Calories
- 10g fat
- 20g protein

Teriyaki Chicken Drumsticks with Salad Greens

Difficulty: Easy

Preparation Time: 11 minutes

Cooking Time: 20 minutes

Servings: 6

Ingredients:

* 6 chicken drumsticks (3 lean)
* Teriyaki sauce: 1 cup (1 green)
* Salad greens: 1 cup (1/2 green)
* Sesame seeds and green onion, for garnish (1/2 green)

Directions:

1. Let the air-fryer preheat to 360F.

2. Pour teriyaki sauce in a big zip lock bag, add in chicken drumsticks.

3. Mix them so well coated. Let it marinate for half an hour.

4. Put drumsticks in a single layer in the air fryer basket, let it cook for 20 minutes.

5. Shake the basket multiple times for even cooking.

6. Top with green onions, sesame seeds, and serve with the side of salad greens.

Nutrition:

* 163 Calories
* 16g Protein
* 7g Fat

Air Fryer Rotisserie Chicken

Difficulty: Average

Preparation Time: 11 minutes

Cooking Time: 60 minutes

Servings: 6

Ingredients:

* Paprika: 1 tsp. (1/4 condiment)
* One chicken (1 lean)
* Dried basil: 1 tsp. (1/4 green)
* Dried oregano: 1 tsp. (1/4 green)
* Pepper: 1/2 tsp. (1/4 condiment)
* Salt: 1 and 1/2 tsp. (1/4 condiment)
* Chopped cilantro and scallions (1/4 green)

Directions:

1. Let the air fryer preheat to 360F.

2. Incorporate all the spices and rub them all over the chicken.

3. Put the chicken in the air fryer and let it cook at 360F for half an hour or more, if required.

4. Serve with salad greens and top with scallions and cilantro.

Nutrition:

* 391 Calories
* 34g Protein
* 27g Fat

Sriracha-honey Chicken Wings

Difficulty: Easy

Preparation Time: 21 minutes

Cooking Time: 15 minutes

Servings: 2

Ingredients:

* Soy sauce: 1 and 1/2 tablespoons (1/4 condiment)
* Chicken wings: 4 cups (2 lean)
* Sriracha sauce: 2 tablespoons (1/4 condiment)
* Butter: 1 tablespoon (1/2 healthy fat)
* 1/2 cup honey (1/2 healthy fat)
* Juice of half lime (1/4 condiment)
* Scallion's cilantro, and chives for garnish (1/4 green)

Directions:

1. Let the air fryer pre-heat to 360 degrees F.

2. Put the chicken wings in an air fryer basket, cook for half an hour, flip the wings every seven minutes, and cook thoroughly.

3. Meanwhile, in a saucepan, add all the ingredients of the sauce and simmer for three minutes.

4. Take out the chicken wings and coat them in sauce well.

5. Garnish with scallions. Serve with a microgreen salad.

Nutrition:

* 207 Calories
* 22g Proteins
* 15g Fat

Smothered Chicken Thighs

Difficulty: Average

Preparation Time: 8 minutes

Cooking Time: 30 minutes

Servings: 4

Ingredients:

- 8-ounce of chicken thighs (3 lean)
- 1 tsp paprika (1/8 condiment)
- 1 pinch salt (1/8 condiment)
- Mushrooms: 1/2 cup (1/2 healthy fat)

Directions:

1. Let the air fryer preheat to 400F

2. Chicken thighs season with paprika, salt, and pepper on both sides.

3. Place the thighs in the air fryer and cook for 20 minutes.

4. Meanwhile, sauté the mushroom.

5. Take out the thighs from the air fryer serve with sautéed mushrooms and onions.

6. And serve with chopped scallions and on the side of salad greens

Nutrition:

- 466.3 Calories
- 32g Fat
- 41g Protein

Mixed Vegetables with Chicken

Difficulty: Easy

Preparation Time: 11 minutes

Cooking Time: 20 minutes

Servings: 2

Ingredients:

- Chicken breast: 4 cups, cubed pieces (1 lean)
- Half zucchini chopped (1/2 green)
- Italian seasoning: 1 tablespoon (1/4 condiment)
- Bell pepper chopped: 1/2 cup (1/2 green)
- Clove of garlic pressed (1/4 condiment)
- Broccoli florets: 1/2 cup (1/2 green)
- Olive oil: 2 tablespoons (1/4 condiment)
- Half teaspoon of chili powder, garlic powder, pepper, salt, (1/4 condiment)

Directions:

1. Let the air fryer heat to 400 F and dice the vegetables

2. In a bowl, add the seasoning, oil and add vegetables, chicken and toss well

3. Place chicken and vegetables in the air fryer, and cook for ten minutes, toss halfway through, cook in batches.

4. Make sure the veggies are charred and the chicken is cooked through.

5. Serve hot.

Nutrition

- 230 Calories
- 26g Protein
- 10g Fat

Mexican-Style Air Fryer Stuffed Chicken Breasts

Difficulty: Average

Preparation Time: 14 minutes

Cooking Time: 10 minutes

Servings: 2

Ingredients:

- Olive oil: 2 teaspoons (1/8 condiment)
- One chicken breast (skinless, boneless) (1 lean)
- Chili powder: 4 tsp., divided (1/8 condiment)
- Chipotle flakes: 2 tsp. (1/8 condiment)
- Half bell pepper, sliced (1/2 green)
- Mexican oregano: 2 tsp. (1/4 green)
- Salt and pepper, to taste (1/8 condiment)
- Ground cumin: 4 tsp., divided (1/8 condiment)
- Half juice of a lime (1/8 condiment)
- One jalapeno pepper, sliced (1/4 green)

Directions:

1. In a bowl, add two tsp of cumin and two tsp. of chili powder, mix well

2. Let the air fryer Preheat to 400 F

3. Pound the chicken breast until 1/4 inch of thickness remains.

4. In a bowl, mix remaining chili powder, chipotle flakes, salt, oregano, remaining cumin, and pepper. Rub this spice mix all over the chicken.

5. Put half the bell pepper, jalapeno, and onion in the breast half. Roll the chicken around it and secure it with large toothpicks.

6. Add olive oil on breast rolls and coat in the cumin-chili mixture.

7. Add chicken breast to air fryer and cook for six minutes.

8. Flip the breast rolls and cook for five minutes more until the chicken's temperature reaches 165 F.

9. Drizzle lime juice on top of breast rolls and serve hot.

Nutrition:

- 185.3 calories
- 14g protein
- 8.5g fat

Air-Fried Grilled BBQ Chicken

Difficulty: Easy
Preparation Time: 19 minutes
Cooking Time: 12 minutes
Servings: 2
Ingredients:

- Chicken Steaks: 2 pieces (1 lean)
- Sea salt: 1 tsp. (1/4 condiment)
- 1 tsp. olive oil (1/4 condiment)
- Black Pepper 1/2 teaspoon (1/4 condiment)
- Blue Cheese & Butter (1/2 healthy fat)

Directions:

1. While making steak, the most important thing is to let the meat rest at room temperature for 30 minutes, for the minimum.

2. Start the recipe by letting the air fryer heat. For making any kind of steak, you should always preheat the air fryer. Therefore, the meat would come out well, then turn the air fryer on at 400 F for 5 minutes.

3. Rub the steak with butter or herb-infused olive oil and sprinkle with sea salt and black pepper.

4. Place the stakes for 6 minutes in the air fryer, then turn over again for almost 6 minutes.

5. Yet again, rest the steak for the very least for 5 minutes, and then slice it.

6. The steaks will keep on cooking, even after it is done cooking.

7. Only combine the butter and the Blue Cheese in a small bowl to mix to make the cheese. You can serve the steak as you like.

8. Put the butter in a wrap and rolled it tightly, it would appear like a roll, keep it refrigerated, and cut off a few bits for each portion.

Nutrition:

- 200 Calories
- 20g Proteins
- 5g Fat

Crispy Korean Air Fried Chicken Wings

Difficulty: Easy
Preparation Time: 7 minutes
Cooking Time: 30 minutes
Servings: 4
Ingredients:

- Chicken wings: 4 cups (2 lean)
- Onion powder: 1 tsp (1/8 condiment)
- Corn starch: ¾ cup (1/8 condiment)
- Garlic powder: 1 tsp (1/8 condiment)
- Salt: ½ tsp (1/8 condiment)
- Korean Air Fried Chicken Sauce (1/8 condiment)
- Soy sauce: 1 Tbsp. (1/8 condiment)
- Korean chili paste: 2 Tbsp. (1/8 condiment)
- Honey: 3 Tbsp. (1 healthy fat)
- Ginger minced: 1 tsp (1/8 condiment)
- Garlic minced: 1 tsp (1/8 condiment)
- Brown sugar: 2 Tbsp. (1/2 healthy fat)
- 1/2 tsp. salts (1/8 condiment)

Directions:

1. Wash and pat dry the chicken wings, in a bowl, add ½ tsp of salt, onion powder, and garlic powder and then add chicken wings and coat them well

2. Then coat the wings in corn starch. And put them in the air fryer.

3. Let the wings cook at 390 F for half an hour. Rotate every ten minutes.

4. Korean Sauce

5. In a saucepan, over medium flame, add all ingredients and let it boil and simmer for five minutes. Turn the heat off

6.   Add cooked wings to the sauce and coat well.

7.   Serve with steamed vegetables.

Nutrition:

- 340 Calories
- 23g Protein
- 19g Fat

Air Fryer Grilled Chicken

Difficulty: Easy

Preparation Time: 11 minutes

Cooking Time: 20 minutes

Servings: 3

Ingredients:

- Chicken tenders: 4 cups (2 lean)

Marinade:

- Honey: 2 Tbsp. (1/8 condiment)
- Olive oil: 1/4 cup (1/8 condiment)
- White vinegar: 2 Tbsp. (1/8 condiment)
- Water: 2 Tbsp. (1/8 condiment)
- Half teaspoon salts (1/8 condiment)
- Garlic powder: 1 tsp. (1/8 condiment)
- Half teaspoon of paprika (1/8 condiment)
- Half teaspoon crushed red pepper (1/2 green)

Directions:

1.   Incorporate all ingredients of the marinade and mix well.

2.   Then add the chicken mix to coat. Cover with plastic wrap and marinate in the refrigerator for half an hour.

3.   Put chicken tenders in the air fryer basket in one even layer.

4.   Cook for 3 minutes at 390 F. flip the tenders over and cook for five minutes more or until chicken is completely cooked through.

5.   Serve with the side of salad greens.

Nutrition:

- 230 calories
- 14g fat
- 20g protein

Crispy Parmesan Buttermilk Chicken Tenders

Difficulty: Average

Preparation Time: 13 minutes

Cooking Time: 18 minutes

Servings: 4

Ingredients:

- 1/2 cup of all-purpose flour (1/2 condiment)
- Buttermilk: 3/4 cup (1/2 healthy fat)
- Chicken breasts: 2, boneless, skinless (1 lean)
- Kosher salt: 3/4 teaspoon, divided (1/4 condiment)
- Grated Parmesan cheese: 1/4 cup (1/2 healthy fat)
- Black Pepper: 3/4 teaspoon, divided (1/4 condiment)
- Worcestershire sauce: 1 and 1/2 teaspoons, divided (1/4 condiment)
- Smoked paprika: half teaspoon, divided (1/4 condiment)
- Oil spray (1/4 condiment)
- Whole wheat breadcrumbs: 1 and 1/2 cups (1/2 healthy fat)
- One large egg (1/2 healthy fat)

Directions:

1.   Cut the chicken into tenders.

2.   In a bowl, add buttermilk and Worcestershire sauce (half of it), salt, and half of paprika and pepper. Add this mix in a zip lock bag with chicken tenders and let it marinate for six hours or more.

3.   In a bowl, add melted butter and breadcrumbs, parmesan cheese and combine well

4.   Whisk the egg with the remaining Worcestershire sauce.

5.   In another bowl, add the smoked paprika, pepper, flour, and salt.

6.   Coat the tenders in flour mixture, then in egg again, then in breadcrumbs mixture.

7.   Let the air fryer preheat to 400 F. put the breaded tenders in the air fryer basket in one even layer.

8.   Cook at 400 F for 13-15 minutes, flip the chicken after half time.

9. Serve with sauces and microgreen

Nutrition:

- 350 Calories
- 14g Fat
- 23g Protein

Air Fryer Low Carb Chicken Bites

Difficulty: Easy

Preparation Time: 14 minutes

Cooking Time: 10 minutes

Servings: 3

Ingredients:

- Chicken breast: 2 cups (1 lean)
- Kosher salt & pepper to taste (1/2 condiment)
- Smashed potatoes: 1 cup (1/3 healthy fat)
- Scallions: ¼ cup (1/2 green)
- One Egg beat (1/3 healthy fat)
- Whole wheat breadcrumbs: 1 cup (1/3 healthy fat)

Directions:

1. Boil the chicken until soft. Shred the chicken with the help of a fork. Add the smashed potatoes, scallions to the shredded chicken. Season with kosher salt and pepper. Coat with egg and then in bread crumbs. Put in the air fryer, and cook for 8 minutes at 380F. Or until golden brown. Serve warm.

Nutrition:

- 234 Calories
- 25g protein
- 9g fat

Lemon Pepper Chicken

Difficulty: Easy

Preparation Time: 9 minutes

Cooking Time: 16 minutes

Servings: 2

Ingredients:

- Two Lemons rind, juice, and zest (1/2 condiment)
- One Chicken Breast (1 lean)
- Minced Garlic: 1 Tsp (1/8 condiment)
- Black Peppercorns: 2 tbsp. (1/8 condiment)

- Chicken Seasoning: 1 Tbsp. (1/8 condiment)
- Salt & pepper to taste (1/8 condiment)

Directions:

1. Let the air fryer preheat to 180C. In a large aluminum foil, add all the seasonings along with lemon rind. Add salt and pepper to the chicken and rub the seasonings all over the chicken breast. Put the chicken in aluminum foil. And fold it tightly. Flatten the chicken inside foil with a rolling pin. Put it in the air fryer and cook at 180 C for 15 minutes. Serve hot.

Nutrition:

- 140 Calories
- 13g Protein
- 2g Fat

Air-fried Chicken Pie

Difficulty: Average

Preparation Time: 11 minutes

Cooking Time: 30 minutes

Servings: 2

Ingredients:

- Puff pastry: 2 sheets (1/2 healthy fat)
- Chicken thighs: 2 pieces, cut into cubes (1 lean)
- Small potatoes: 2, chopped (1/2 healthy fat)
- Mushrooms: 1/4 cup (1/2 healthy fat)
- Light soya sauce (1/4 condiment)
- 1 carrot, chopped (1 green)
- Black pepper to taste (1/4 condiment)
- Worcestershire sauce: to taste (1/4 condiment)
- Salt to taste (1/4 condiment)
- Italian mixed dried herbs (1/2 green)
- Garlic powder: a pinch (1/4 condiment)
- Plain flour: 2 tbsp. (1/4 healthy fat)
- Milk, as required (1/4 healthy fat)
- Melted butter (/8 healthy fat)

Directions:

1. Incorporate light soya sauce and pepper, add the chicken cubes and coat well.

2.   In a pan over medium heat, sauté carrot, potatoes, and onion. Add some water, if required, to cook the vegetables.

3.   Add the chicken cubes and mushrooms and cook them too.

4.   Stir in black pepper, salt, Worcestershire sauce, garlic powder, and dried herbs.

5.   When the chicken is cooked through, add some of the flour and mix well.

6.   Add in the milk and let the vegetables simmer until tender.

7.   Place one piece of puff pastry in the baking tray of the air fryer, poke holes with a fork.

8.   Add on top the cooked chicken filling and eggs and puff pastry on top with holes. Cut the excess pastry off. Glaze with oil spray or melted butter

9.   Air fry at 180 F for six minutes or until it becomes golden brown.

10.   Serve with microgreens.

Nutrition:

- 224 calories
- 20g protein
- 18g fat

Air Fryer Nashville Hot Chicken with Spinach Salad

Difficulty: Average

Preparation Time: 11 minutes

Cooking Time: 25 minutes

Servings: 8

Ingredients:

- Buttermilk: 2 cups (1/2 healthy fat)
- Chicken thighs(bone-in): 8 (3 lean)
- Cayenne pepper: 1 tsp. (1/8 condiment)
- Hot sauce: 1/4 cup (1/8 condiment)
- Garlic powder: 2 Tbsp. (1/8 condiment)
- Salt: 1 tsp. (1/8 condiment)
- Low-fat butter: 1/2 cup (1/2 healthy fat)
- Flour: 2 cups (1/8 condiment)
- Black pepper: 1 tsp. (1/8 condiment)
- Old bay: 1 tsp. (1/2 green)
- Paprika: 1 tsp. (1/8 condiment)

Directions:

1.   In a mixing bowl, add hot sauce and buttermilk, mix it well, then add chicken pieces.

2.   Marinate in the refrigerator for 1 to 24 hours.

3.   In a bowl, add garlic powder, flour, salt, black pepper, paprika, cayenne pepper, and old bay. Mix well.

4.   Always cook the chicken in a single layer, in the air fryer

5.   Take chicken out from buttermilk, coat in the flour mix. Situate the chicken rest on a cooling rack for 15 minutes before putting it in the air fryer.

6.   Place the breaded chicken in the air fryer, leaving room between the pieces.

7.   Cook for 25 minutes, at 390 F. after halftime, take the basket out and spray the chicken with olive oil

8.   This step is optional. Mix two tbsp. Of hot sauce with melted butter. Brush the cooked crispy chicken with it.

9.   Serve with the spinach salad.

Nutrition:

- 333 calories
- 20g Fat
- 26g protein

Air Fryer Spicy Chicken & Vegetables

Difficulty: Average

Preparation Time: 8 minutes

Cooking Time: 20 minutes

Servings: 2

Ingredients:

Spiced Chicken

- Chicken breasts: 2 skinless, boneless (1 lean)
- Onion powder: 1/2 tsp. (1/8 condiment)
- Olive oil: 1/2 Tbsp. (1/8 condiment)
- Chili powder: 1 tsp. (1/8 condiment)
- Cumin: 1/4 tsp. (1/8 condiment)
- Paprika: 1/2 tsp. (1/8 condiment)
- Salt: 1/2 tsp. (1/8 condiment)
- Garlic powder: 1/2 tsp. (1/8 condiment)
- Pepper: 1/2 tsp. (1/8 condiment)

Vegetables

- Carrots: 2-3 large (1 green)
- Olive oil: 1/2 Tbsp. (1/8 condiment)
- Chopped scallions (1 green)
- Pinch of salt (1/8 condiment)

Directions:

1. Let the air fryer preheat to 325 F

2. In a big bowl, add all chicken spices and make a spice mix. Then add chicken breasts with half tbsp. of olive oil and coat well. Set it aside.

3. Cut the vegetables according to your preference. Cut onions in layers, and separate each layer, coat all the vegetables with half tbsp. of olive oil and salt

4. Lay vegetables in the air fryer first, then add chicken on top—Cook for almost 35 minutes or more. Flip the chicken halfway through and toss the vegetables.

5. Serve hot.

Nutrition:

- 344 Calories
- 28g Protein
- 11g Fat

Seafood Recipes

Fish Finger Sandwich

Difficulty: Average
Preparation Time: 10 minutes
Cooking Time: 9 minutes
Servings: 4
Ingredients

- Greek yogurt: 1 tbsp. (1/2 healthy fat)
- Cod fillets: 4, without skin (2 lean)
- Flour: 2 tbsp. (1/4 healthy fat)
- Whole-wheat breadcrumbs: 5 tbsp. (1/4 healthy fat)
- Kosher salt and pepper, to taste (1/4 condiment)
- Capers: 10–12 (1/2 healthy fat)
- Lemon juice (1/4 condiment)

Direction

1. Let the air fryer preheat.
2. Sprinkle kosher salt and pepper on the cod fillets, and coat in flour, then in breadcrumbs
3. Spray the fryer basket with oil. Put the cod fillets in the basket.
4. Cook for 15 minutes at 200 C.
5. In the meantime, blend with Greek yogurt, lemon juice, and capers until well combined.
6. On a bun, add cooked fish with pea puree. Add lettuce and tomato.

Nutrition:

- 240 Calories
- 12g Fat
- 20g Protein

Air Fryer Catfish with Cajun Seasoning

Difficulty: Easy
Preparation Time: 5 minutes
Cooking Time: 27 minutes
Servings: 4
Ingredients

- Cajun seasoning: 3 teaspoons (1/2 condiment)
- Cornmeal: 3/4 cup (1/2 healthy fat)
- 4 catfish fillets (2 lean)

Direction

1. In a zip lock bag, add Cajun seasoning and cornmeal
2. Wash and pat dry the catfish fillets. Add them to the zip lock bag.
3. Coat well the fillets with seasoning
4. Put catfish fillets in the air fryer and cook for 15 minutes at 390 F, turn fillets halfway through. To get a golden color on the fillets, cook for five more minutes.
5. Serve with lemon wedges and spicy tartar sauce.

Nutrition

- 324 Calories
- 14g Fat
- 26.3g Protein

Air Fryer Crispy Fish Sandwich

Difficulty: Easy
Preparation Time: 11 minutes
Cooking Time: 12 minutes
Servings: 2
Ingredients

- Cod :2 fillets (1 lean)
- All-purpose flour: 2 tablespoons (1/4 condiment)
- Pepper: 1/4 teaspoon (1/8 condiment)
- Lemon juice: 1 tablespoon (1/4 condiment)
- Salt: 1/4 teaspoon (1/8 condiment)
- Garlic powder: half teaspoon (1/8 condiment)
- One egg (1/2 healthy fat)
- Mayo: half tablespoon (1/4 healthy fat)
- Whole wheat bread crumbs: half cup (1/2 healthy fat)

Direction

1. In a bowl, add salt, flour, pepper, and garlic powder.
2. In a separate bowl, add lemon juice, mayo, and egg.
3. In another bowl, add the breadcrumbs.

4. Coat the fish in flour, then in egg, then in breadcrumbs.

5. With cooking oil, spray the basket and put the fish in the basket. Also, spray the fish with cooking oil.

6. Cook at 400 F for ten minutes. This fish is soft, be careful if you flip.

Nutrition:

- 218 Calories
- 12g Fat
- 22g Protein

Shrimp Spring Rolls

Difficulty: Average

Preparation Time: 9 minutes

Cooking Time: 25 minutes

Servings: 4

Ingredients

- Deveined raw shrimp: half cup chopped(peeled) (1 lean)
- Olive oil: 2 and 1/2 tbsp. (1/8 condiment)
- Matchstick carrots: 1 cup (1/2 green)
- Slices of red bell pepper: 1 cup (1/2 green)
- Red pepper: 1/4 teaspoon(crushed) (1/4 green)
- Shredded cabbage: 2 cups (1 green)
- Lime juice: 1 tablespoon (1/8 condiment)
- Sweet chili sauce: half cup (1/8 condiment)
- Fish sauce: 2 teaspoons (1/8 condiment)
- Eight spring roll(wrappers) (1 healthy fat)

Direction

1. In a skillet, add one and a half tbsp. of olive, until smoking lightly. Stir in bell pepper, cabbage, carrots, and cook for two minutes. Turn off the heat, take out in a dish and cool for five minutes.

2. In a bowl, add shrimp, lime juice, cabbage mixture, crushed red pepper, and fish sauce. Mix well

3. Lay spring roll wrappers on a plate. Add 1/4 cup of filling in the middle of each wrapper. Fold tightly with water. Brush the olive oil over folded rolls.

4. Put spring rolls in the air fryer basket and cook for 6 to 7 minutes at 390°F until light brown and crispy.

5. You may serve with sweet chili sauce.

Nutrition:

- 180 Calories
- 9g Fat
- 17g Protein

Breaded Air Fried Shrimp with Bang-Bang Sauce

Difficulty: Difficult

Preparation Time: 9 minutes

Cooking Time: 22 minutes

Servings: 4

Ingredients

- Whole wheat bread crumbs: 3/4 cup (1/2 healthy fat)
- Raw shrimp: 4 cups, deveined, peeled (2 lean)
- Flour: half cup (1/8 condiment)
- Paprika: 1 tsp (1/8 condiment)
- Chicken Seasoning, to taste (1/8 condiment)
- 2 tbsp. of one egg white (1/2 healthy fat)
- Kosher salt and pepper to taste (1/8 condiment)

Bang-Bang Sauce

- Sweet chili sauce: 1/4 cup (1/8 condiment)
- Plain Greek yogurt: 1/3 cup (1/3 healthy fat)
- Sriracha: 2 tbsp. (1/8 condiment)

Direction

1. Let the Air Fryer preheat to 400 degrees.

2. Add the seasonings to shrimp and coat well.

3. In three separate bowls, add flour, bread crumbs, and egg whites.

4. First coat the shrimp in flour, dab lightly in egg whites, then in the bread crumbs.

5. With cooking oil, spray the shrimp.

6. Place the shrimps in an air fryer, cook for four minutes, turn the shrimp over, and cook for another four minutes. Serve with micro green and bang-bang sauce.

Bang-Bang Sauce

7. Incorporate all the ingredients and serve.

Nutrition:

- 229 calories

- 10g fat
- 22g protein

Air Fryer Lemon Pepper Shrimp

Difficulty: Average

Preparation Time: 6 minutes

Cooking Time: 11 minutes

Servings: 2

Ingredients

- Raw shrimp: 1 and 1/2 cup peeled, deveined (1 lean)
- Olive oil: 1/2 tablespoon (1/4 condiment)
- Garlic powder: ¼ tsp (1/8 condiment)
- Lemon pepper: 1 tsp (1/4 condiment)
- Paprika: ¼ tsp (1/8 condiment)
- Juice of one lemon (1/4 condiment)

Direction

1. Let the air fryer preheat to 400 F
2. In a bowl, mix lemon pepper, olive oil, paprika, garlic powder, and lemon juice. Mix well. Add shrimps and coat well
3. Add shrimps in the air fryer, cook for 6 or 8 minutes and top with lemon slices and serve

Nutrition:

- 237 Calories
- 6g Fat
- 36g Protein

Air Fryer Garlic-Lime Shrimp Kebabs

Difficulty: Easy

Preparation Time: 5 minutes

Cooking Time: 19 minutes

Servings: 2

Ingredients

- 1 lime (1/4 condiment)
- Raw shrimp: 1 cup (1 lean)
- Salt: 1/8 teaspoon (1/4 condiment)
- 1 clove of garlic (1/4 condiment)
- Freshly ground black pepper (1/4 condiment)

Direction

1. In water, let wooden skewers soak for 20 minutes.
2. Let the Air fryer preheat to 350F.

3. In a bowl, mix shrimp, minced garlic, lime juice, kosher salt, and pepper
4. Add shrimp on skewers.
5. Place skewers in the air fryer, and cook for 8 minutes. Turn halfway over.
6. Top with cilantro and your favorite dip.

Nutrition:

- 76 Calories
- 13g Protein
- 9g fat

Air Fryer Sushi Roll

Difficulty: Difficult

Preparation Time: 91 minutes

Cooking Time: 9 minutes

Servings: 3

Ingredients

For the Kale Salad

- Rice vinegar: half teaspoon (1/8 condiment)
- Chopped kale: one and a 1/2 cups (1/2 green)
- Garlic powder:1/8 teaspoon (1/8 condiment)
- Sesame seeds: 1 tablespoon (1/4 healthy fat)
- Toasted sesame oil: 3/4 teaspoon (1/8 condiment)
- Ground ginger: 1/4 teaspoon (1/8 condiment)
- Soy sauce: 3/4 teaspoon (1/8 condiment)

Sushi Rolls

- Half avocado - sliced (1/2 healthy fat)
- Cooked Sushi Rice - cooled (1 healthy fat)
- Whole wheat breadcrumbs: half cup (1/2 healthy fat)
- Sushi: 3 sheets (1 lean)

Direction

Make the Kale Salad

1. In a bowl, add vinegar, garlic powder, kale, soy sauce, sesame oil, and ground ginger. With your hands, mix with sesame seeds and set them aside.

Sushi Rolls

2. Lay a sheet of sushi on a flat surface. With damp fingertips, add a tablespoon of rice, and

spread it on the sheet. Cover the sheet with rice, leaving half-inch space at one end.

3.   Add kale salad with avocado slices. Roll up the sushi, use water if needed.

4.   Add the breadcrumbs in a bowl. Coat the sushi roll with Sriracha Mayo, then in breadcrumbs.

5.   Add the rolls to the air fryer. Cook for ten minutes at 390 F, shake the basket halfway through.

6.   Take out from the fryer, and let them cool, then cut with a sharp knife.

7.   Serve with soy sauce.

Nutrition:

*   369 Calories
*   13.9g Fat
*   26g Protein

Easy Shrimp PO' Boy

Difficulty: Easy
Preparation Time: 19 minutes
Cooking Time: 9 minutes
Servings: 4
Ingredients

*   Iceberg lettuce: 2 cups shredded (1 green)
*   Shrimp:4 cups, deveined (2 lean)
*   Buttermilk: 1/4 cup (1/4 healthy fat)
*   Fish Fry Coating: 1/2 cup (1/4 condiment)
*   Creole Seasoning: 1 teaspoon (1/8 condiment)
*   Eight slices of tomato (1/2 green)

Remoulade Sauce

*   Creole Seasoning: half tsp. (1/8 condiment)
*   Mayo: half cup(reduced-fat) (1/2 healthy fat)
*   Half lemon's juice (1/8 condiment)
*   Dijon mustard: 1 tsp (1/8 condiment)
*   Worcestershire: 1 tsp (1/8 condiment)
*   Minced garlic: one tsp. (1/8 condiment)
*   One green onion chopped (1/4 condiment)
*   Hot sauce: one tsp

Direction

Remoulade Sauce

1.   Mix all ingredients in a bowl. Chill in Refrigerator.

Shrimp

2.   In a zip lock bag, add buttermilk and Creole seasoning with shrimp and mix well, marinate for half an hour.

3.   With cooking oil, spray the air fryer basket. Place the shrimp in the air fryer basket.

4.   Spray the shrimp with olive oil.

5.   Cook at 400 F for five minutes. Flip the shrimps over, and cook for extra five minutes.

6.   Add the remoulade sauce on whole-wheat bread. Then add tomato slices and lettuce on top, then the shrimp. Enjoy

Nutrition:

*   247 Calories
*   19.3g fat
*   24.7g protein

Air Fryer Lemon Garlic Shrimp

Difficulty: Average
Preparation Time: 6 minutes
Cooking Time: 12 minutes
Servings: 2
Ingredients

*   Olive oil: 1 Tbsp. (1/4 condiment)
*   Small shrimp: 4 cups, peeled, tails removed (2 lean)
*   One lemon juice and zest (1/4 condiment)
*   Parsley: 1/4 cup sliced (1/4 green)
*   Red pepper flakes(crushed): 1 pinch (1/4 condiment)
*   Four cloves of grated garlic (1/8 condiment)
*   Sea salt: 1/4 teaspoon (1/8 condiment)

Direction

1.   Let air fryer heat to 400F

2.   Mix olive oil, lemon zest, red pepper flakes, shrimp, kosher salt, and garlic in a bowl and coat the shrimp well.

3.   Place shrimps in the air fryer basket, coat with oil spray.

4.   Cook at 400 F for 8 minutes. Toss the shrimp halfway through

5.   Serve with lemon slices and parsley.

Nutrition:

*   140 Calories
*   18g Fat

- 20g Protein

Air Fryer Scallops with Tomato Cream Sauce

Difficulty: Average

Preparation Time: 5 minutes

Cooking Time: 10 minutes

Servings: 2

Ingredients

- Sea scallops eight jumbo (4 lean)
- Tomato Paste: 1 tbsp. (1/4 condiment)
- Chopped fresh basil 1 tablespoon (1/2 green)
- 3/4 cup of low-fat Whipping Cream (1/2 healthy fat)
- Kosher salt half teaspoon (1/4 condiment)
- Ground Freshly black pepper half teaspoon (1/4 condiment)
- Minced garlic 1 teaspoon (1/4 condiment)
- Frozen Spinach, thawed half cup (1/2 green)

Direction

1. Take a seven-inch pan(heatproof) and add spinach in a single layer at the bottom
2. Rub olive oil on both sides of scallops, season with kosher salt and pepper.
3. on top of the spinach, place the seasoned scallops
4. Put the pan in the air fryer and cook for ten minutes at 350F, until scallops are cooked completely, and the internal temperature reaches 135F.
5. Serve immediately.

Nutrition:

- 259 Calories
- 19g Protein
- 13g Fat

Quick & Easy Air Fryer Salmon

Difficulty: Easy

Preparation Time: 6 minutes

Cooking Time: 13 minutes

Servings: 4

Ingredients

- Lemon pepper seasoning: 2 teaspoons (1/4 condiment)
- Salmon: 4 cups (2 lean)
- Olive oil: one tablespoon (1/4 condiment)
- Seafood seasoning: 2 teaspoons (1/4 condiment)
- Half lemon's juice (1/4 condiment)
- Garlic powder:1 teaspoon (1/8 condiment)
- Kosher salt to taste (1/8 condiment)

Direction

1. In a bowl, add one tbsp. of olive oil and half lemon juice.
2. Pour this mixture over salmon and rub. Leave the skin on salmon. It will come off when cooked.
3. Rub the salmon with kosher salt and spices.
4. Put parchment paper in the air fryer basket. Put the salmon in the air fryer.
5. Cook at 360 F for ten minutes. Cook until inner salmon temperature reaches 140 F.
6. Let the salmon rest five minutes before serving.
7. Serve with salad greens and lemon wedges.

Nutrition:

- 132 Calories
- 7.4g fat
- 22g protein

Sriracha & Honey Tossed Calamari

Difficulty: Easy

Preparation Time: 9 minutes

Cooking Time: 20 minutes

Servings: 2

Ingredients

- Club soda: 1 cup (1/2 condiment)
- Sriracha: 1-2 Tbsp. (1/4 condiment)
- Calamari tubes: 2 cups (1 lean)
- Flour: 1 cup (1/2 healthy fat)
- Pinches of salt, freshly ground black pepper, red pepper flakes, and red pepper (1/4 condiment)
- Honey: 1/2 cup (1/2 healthy fat)

Direction

1. Cut the calamari tubes into rings. Submerge them with club soda. Let it rest for ten minutes.

2. In the meantime, in a bowl, add freshly ground black pepper, flour, red pepper, and kosher salt and mix well.

3. Drain the calamari and pat dry with a paper towel. Coat the calamari well in the flour mix and set aside.

4. Spray oil in the air fryer basket and put calamari in one single layer.

5. Cook at 375 for 11 minutes. Toss the rings twice while cooking. Meanwhile, to make sauce honey, red pepper flakes, and sriracha in a bowl, well.

6. Take calamari out from the basket, mix with sauce, cook for another two minutes more. Serve with salad green.

Nutrition

- 252 Calories
- 38g Fat
- 41g Protein

Air Fryer Parmesan Shrimp

Difficulty: Average
Preparation Time: 6 minutes
Cooking Time: 12 minutes
Servings: 4
Ingredients

- Olive oil: 2 tablespoons (1/2 condiment)
- Jumbo cooked shrimp: 8 cups, peeled, deveined (4 lean)
- Parmesan cheese: 2/3 cup(grated) (1/2 healthy fat)
- Pepper: 1 teaspoon (1/4 condiment)
- 4 cloves of minced garlic (1/2 condiment)
- Oregano: 1/2 teaspoon (1/4 green)
- Basil: 1 teaspoon (1/4 green)
- Lemon wedges (1/2 condiment)

Direction

1. Mix parmesan cheese, onion powder, oregano, olive oil, garlic, basil, and pepper in a bowl. Coat the shrimp in this mixture.

2. Spray oil on the air fryer basket, put shrimp in it.

3. Cook for ten minutes, at 350 F, or until browned.

4. Drizzle the lemon on shrimps before serving with a microgreen salad.

Nutrition:

- 198 Calories
- 13g Fat
- 12.7g Protein

Healthy Air Fryer Tuna Patties

Difficulty: Easy
Preparation Time: 15 minutes
Cooking Time: 11 minutes
Servings: 10
Ingredients

- Whole wheat breadcrumbs: half cup (1/4 healthy fat)
- Fresh tuna: 4 cups, diced (2 lean)
- Lemon zest (1/4 condiment)
- Lemon juice: 1 Tablespoon (1/4 condiment)
- 1 egg (1/4 healthy fat)
- Grated parmesan cheese: 3 Tablespoons (1/4 healthy fat)
- One chopped stalk celery (1 green)
- Garlic powder: half teaspoon (1/4 condiment)
- Dried herbs: half teaspoon (1/4 green)
- Salt to taste (1/8 condiment)
- Freshly ground black pepper (1/8 condiment)

Direction

1. In a bowl, add lemon zest, bread crumbs, salt, pepper, celery, eggs, dried herbs, lemon juice, garlic powder, parmesan cheese, and onion. Mix everything. Then add in tuna gently. Shape into patties. If the mixture is too loose, cool in the refrigerator.

2. Add air fryer baking paper in the air fryer basket. Spray the baking paper with cooking spray.

3. Spray the patties with oil.

4. Cook for ten minutes at 360°F. Turn the patties halfway over.

5. Serve with lemon slices and microgreens.

Nutrition:

- 214 Calories
- 15g Fat
- 22g Protein

Easy Shrimp Egg Rolls

Difficulty: Average

Preparation Time: 24 minutes

Cooking Time: 19 minutes

Servings: 6

Ingredients

- 2-3 cloves of minced garlic (1/2 condiment)
- 12-14 egg roll wrappers (1 healthy fat)
- Raw shrimp (roughly chopped): 4 cups, peeled and deveined (2 lean)
- Coleslaw mix: 3 cups (1 healthy fat)
- Sesame oil: 1 and 1/2 teaspoons (1/8 condiment)
- Soy sauce: 1 tablespoon (1/4 condiment)
- Fish sauce: 1 teaspoon (1/8 condiment)
- Salt, pepper to taste (1/8 condiment)
- Grated ginger: half tsp. (1/8 condiment)
- Two green onions chopped (1 green)
- Water: one cup (1/4 condiment)

Direction

1. In a skillet, add shrimp with garlic, kosher salt, and pepper, spray with cooking oil and sauté until shrimp is pink. Put off the heat and set it aside.

2. In a bowl, add coleslaw mix, cooked shrimp, green onions, fish sauce, soy sauce, sesame oil, and ginger. Mix well.

3. Add two tbsp. Of filling, in each wrapper, seal tightly with water.

4. With cooking oil, spray the air fryer basket. Situate egg rolls in a single layer in the basket. Spray with cooking oil.

5. Cook for 7 minutes at 400 degrees. Flip the rolls, then cook for five minutes more.

6. Serve with micro green salad.

Nutrition:

- 228 calories
- 11g fat
- 20g protein

Air Fryer Southern Style Catfish with Green Beans

Difficulty: Average

Preparation Time: 8 minutes

Cooking Time: 23 minutes

Servings: 2

Ingredients

- Catfish fillets: 2 pieces (1 lean)
- Green beans: half cup, trimmed (1/2 green)
- Honey: 2 teaspoons (1/4 condiment)
- black pepper and salt, to taste (1/4 condiment)
- Crushed red pepper: half tsp. (1/2 green)
- Flour: 1/4 cup (1/4 condiment)
- One egg, lightly beaten (1/2 healthy fat)
- Dill pickle relish: 3/4 teaspoon (1/4 condiment)
- Apple cider vinegar: half tsp (1/4 condiment)
- 1/3 cup whole-wheat breadcrumbs (1/2 healthy fat)
- Mayonnaise: 2 tablespoons (1/4 condiment)
- Dill (1/2 green)
- Lemon wedges (1/4 condiment)

Direction

1. In a bowl, add green beans, spray them with cooking oil. Coat with crushed red pepper, 1/8 teaspoon of kosher salt, and half tsp. Of honey and cook in the air fryer at 400 F until soft and browned, for 12 minutes. Take out from fryer and cover with aluminum foil

2. In the meantime, coat catfish in flour. Then dip in egg to coat, then in breadcrumbs. Place fish in an air fryer basket and spray with cooking oil.

3. Cook for 8 minutes, at 400F.

4. Sprinkle with pepper and salt. In the meantime, mix vinegar, dill, relish, mayonnaise, and honey in a bowl. Serve the sauce with fish and green beans.

Nutrition:

- 243 Calories
- 18g fat
- 33g Protein

Air Fryer Shrimp Tacos

Difficulty: Average
Preparation Time: 16 minutes
Cooking Time: 16 minutes
Servings: 4
Ingredients

- Flour tortillas: 12 (2 healthy fat)
- Avocado sliced: 1 cup (1/4 healthy fat)
- Chipotle chili powder: 1 tsp (1/8 condiment)
- Raw jumbo shrimp: 24 pieces, deveined, peeled, without tail (4 lean)
- Smoked paprika: 1/2 tsp (1/8 condiment)
- Salt: 1/4 tsp (1/8 condiment)
- Olive oil: 1 tbsp. (1/8 condiment)
- Green salsa: ½ cup (1/4 healthy fat)
- Light brown sugar: 1 and 1/2 tsp (1/8 condiment)
- Garlic powder: 1/2 tsp (1/8 condiment)
- Low-fat sour cream: 1/2 cup (1/4 healthy fat)

Direction

1. Let the oven preheat to 400 F and spray the air fryer basket with oil spray.

2. In a bowl, mix chipotle chili powder, salt, brown sugar, smoked paprika, and garlic powder, mix well

3. Pat dry the shrimp, put shrimp in zip lock bag and add the seasonings and toss to coat well

4. Place shrimp in air fryer basket in one even layer, cook for four minutes and flip them overcook for four minutes more

5. For the sauce, mix sour cream and green salsa.

6. Put shrimp in a tortilla, top with sauce, shrimp, sliced avocado serves with lime wedges.

Nutrition:

- 228 Calories
- 18g Fat
- 20g Protein

Roasted Salmon with Fennel Salad

Difficulty: Easy
Preparation Time: 14 minutes
Cooking Time: 9 minutes
Servings: 4
Ingredients

- Skinless and center-cut: 4 salmon fillets (2 lean)
- Lemon juice: 1 teaspoon(fresh) (1/8 condiment)
- Parsley: 2 teaspoons(chopped) (1/4 green)
- Salt: 1 teaspoon, divided (1/8 condiment)
- Olive oil: 2 tablespoons (1/8 condiment)
- Chopped thyme: 1 teaspoon (1/4 green)
- Fennel heads: 4 cups (thinly sliced) (1/4 green)
- One clove of minced garlic (1/8 condiment)
- Fresh dill: 2 tablespoons, chopped (1/4 green)
- Orange juice: 2 tablespoons(fresh) (1/2 healthy fat)
- Greek yogurt: 2/3 cup(reduced-fat) (1/2 healthy fat)

Direction

1. In a bowl, add half teaspoon of salt, parsley, and thyme, mix well. Rub oil over salmon, and sprinkle with thyme mixture.

2. Put salmon fillets in the air fryer basket, cook for ten minutes at 350°F.

3. In the meantime, mix garlic, fennel, orange juice, yogurt, half tsp. of salt, dill, lemon juice in a bowl.

4. Serve with fennel salad.

Nutrition:

- 364 Calories
- 30g Fat
- 38g Protein

Crab Cakes

Difficulty: Average

Preparation Time: 14 minutes

Cooking Time: 19 minutes

Servings: 6

Ingredients

- Crab meat: 4 cups (2 lean)
- 2 eggs (1 healthy fat)
- Whole wheat bread crumbs: ¼ cup (1/2 healthy fat)
- Mayonnaise: 2 tablespoons (1/2 healthy fat)
- Worcestershire sauce: 1 teaspoon (1/4 condiment)
- Old Bay seasoning: 1 and ½ teaspoon (1/4 condiment)
- Dijon mustard: 1 teaspoon (1/4 condiment)
- Black pepper to taste (1/4 condiment)
- Green onion: ¼ cup, chopped (1/4 green)

Direction

1. In a bowl, add Dijon mustard, Old Bay, eggs, Worcestershire, and mayonnaise mix it well. Then add in the chopped green onion and mix.

2. Fold in the crab meat to mayonnaise mix. Then add breadcrumbs, not to over mix.

3. Chill the mix in the refrigerator for at least 60 minutes. Then shape into patties.

4. Let the air-fryer preheat to 350F. Cook for 10 minutes. Flip the patties halfway through.

5. Serve with lemon wedges.

Nutrition:

- 218 Calories
- 13g Fat
- 17g Protein

Vegetable Recipes

Air Fryer Tofu

Difficulty: Easy

Preparation Time: 10 minutes

Cooking Time: 15 minutes

Servings: 4

Ingredients:

- 15 oz extra firm tofu, cut into bite-sized pieces (1 healthy fat)
- 1 tbsp olive oil (1/4 condiment)
- 2 tbsp soy sauce (1/4 condiment)
- 1 garlic clove, minced (1/4 condiment)
- Pepper (1/8 condiment)
- Salt (1/8 condiment)

Directions:

1. Add tofu, garlic, oil, soy sauce, pepper, and salt in a bowl and toss well. Set aside for 15 minutes.

2. Add tofu pieces into the air fryer basket and cook at 370 F for 15 minutes.

3. Serve and enjoy.

Nutrition

- 115 Calories
- 8g Fat
- 9.8g Protein

Spicy Asian Brussels Sprouts

Difficulty: Average

Preparation Time: 10 minutes

Cooking Time: 15 minutes

Servings: 4

Ingredients:

- 1 lb. Brussels sprouts, cut in half (1 green)
- 1 tbsp gochujang (1/2 condiment)
- 1 1/2 tbsp olive oil (1/4 condiment)
- 1/2 tsp salt (1/4 condiment)

Directions:

1. In a bowl, mix olive oil, gochujang, and salt.

2. Add Brussels sprouts into the bowl and toss until well coated.

3. Add Brussels sprouts into the air fryer basket and cook at 360 F for 15 minutes.

4. Serve and enjoy.

Nutrition

- 94 Calories
- 5g Fat
- 4g Protein

Asian Green Beans

Difficulty: Average

Preparation Time: 10 minutes

Cooking Time: 10 minutes

Servings: 2

Ingredients:

- 8 oz green beans (1 green)
- 1 tbsp tamari (1/2 condiment)
- 1 tsp sesame oil (1/2 condiment)

Direction

1. Mix all ingredients into the big bowl and toss well.

2. Add green beans into the air fryer basket and cook at 400 F for 10 minutes.

3. Serve and enjoy.

Nutrition

- 60 Calories
- 2g Fat
- 3g Protein

Cheesy Brussels Sprouts

Difficulty: Easy

Preparation Time: 10 minutes

Cooking Time: 12 minutes

Servings: 4

Ingredients:

- 1 lb. Brussels sprouts, cut stems and halved (1/2 green)
- 1/4 cup parmesan cheese (1/2 healthy fat)
- 1 tbsp olive oil (1/4 condiment)
- 1/4 tsp garlic powder (1/4 condiment)
- Pepper (1/8 condiment)
- Salt (1/8 condiment)

Directions:

1. Preheat the air fryer to 350 F.

2. Toss Brussels sprouts, oil, garlic powder, pepper, and salt into the bowl.

3. Situate Brussels sprouts into the air fryer basket and cook for 12 minutes.

4. Top with cheese and serve.

Nutrition

*   132 Calories
*   7g Fat
*   7g Protein

Healthy Zucchini Patties

Difficulty: Easy

Preparation Time: 10 minutes

Cooking Time: 30 minutes

Servings: 6

Ingredients:

*   1 cup zucchini, shredded and squeeze out all liquid (1/2 green)
*   1 egg, lightly beaten (1/4 healthy fat)
*   1/4 tsp red pepper flakes (1/4 condiment)
*   1/4 cup parmesan cheese, grated (1/4 healthy fat)
*   1/2 tbsp Dijon mustard (1/4 condiment)
*   1/2 tbsp mayonnaise (1/4 healthy fat)
*   1/2 cup breadcrumbs (1/2 healthy fat)
*   Pepper (1/8 condiment)
*   Salt (1/8 condiment)

Directions:

1. Mix all ingredients into the bowl until well combined.

2. Make patties from mixture and place them into the basket and cook at 375 F for 15 minutes.

3. Turn patties and cook for 15 minutes more.

4. Serve and enjoy.

Nutrition

*   80 Calories
*   3g Fat
*   4g Protein

Air Fried Tasty Eggplant

Difficulty: Easy

Preparation Time: 10 minutes

Cooking Time: 12 minutes

Servings: 2

Ingredients:

*   1 eggplant, cut into cubes (1 green)
*   1/4 tsp oregano (1/4 green)
*   1 tbsp olive oil (1/2 condiment)
*   1/2 tsp garlic powder (1/4 condiment)
*   1/4 tsp chili powder (1/4 condiment)

Directions:

1. Incorporate all ingredients into the huge bowl and toss well.

2. Transfer eggplant into the air fryer basket and cook at 390 F for 12 minutes. Stir halfway through.

3. Serve and enjoy.

Nutrition

*   120 Calories
*   7g Fat
*   2g Protein

Garlic Cauliflower Florets

Difficulty: Easy

Preparation Time: 10 minutes

Cooking Time: 20 minutes

Servings: 4

Ingredients:

*   4 cups cauliflower florets (1/2 green)
*   1/2 tsp cumin powder (1/8 condiment)
*   1/2 tsp coriander powder (1/8 condiment)
*   5 garlic cloves, chopped (1/8 condiment)
*   4 tablespoons olive oil (1/8 condiment)
*   1/2 tsp salt (1/8 condiment)

Directions:

1. Add all ingredients into the bowl and toss well.

2. Add cauliflower florets into the air fryer basket and cook at 400 F for 20 minutes. Shake halfway through.

3. Serve and enjoy.

Nutrition

*   153 Calories
*   14g Fat
*   2.3g Protein

Healthy Mushrooms

Difficulty: Easy

Preparation Time: 10 minutes

Cooking Time: 12 minutes

Servings: 2

Ingredients:

- 8 oz mushrooms, clean and cut into quarters (2 healthy fats)
- 1 tbsp fresh parsley, chopped (1/2 green)
- 1 tsp soy sauce (1/4 condiment)
- 1/2 tsp garlic powder (1/4 condiment)
- 1 tbsp olive oil (1/4 condiment)
- Pepper (1/8 condiment)
- Salt (1/8 condiment)

Directions:

1. Add mushrooms and remaining ingredients into the bowl and toss well.

2. Add mushrooms into the air fryer basket and cook at 380 F for 12 minutes. Stir halfway through.

3. Serve and enjoy.

Nutrition

- 90 Calories
- 7g Fat
- 4g Protein

Cheese Stuff Peppers

Difficulty: Average

Preparation Time: 10 minutes

Cooking Time: 8 minutes

Servings: 4

Ingredients:

- 10 jalapeno peppers, halved, remove seeds and stem (4 lean)
- 1/2 cup cheddar cheese (1/4 healthy fat)
- 1/2 cup Monterey jack cheese, shredded (1/4 healthy fat)
- 8 oz cream cheese, softened (1/2 healthy fat)

Directions:

1. In a bowl, mix together Monterey jack cheese and cream cheese.

2. Stuff cheese mixture into jalapeno halved.

3. Place jalapeno pepper into the air fryer basket and cook at 370 F for 8 minutes.

4. Serve and enjoy.

Nutrition

- 365 Calories
- 33g Fat
- 13.2g Protein

Simple Green Beans

Difficulty: Easy

Preparation Time: 10 minutes

Cooking Time: 10 minutes

Servings: 4

Ingredients:

- 2 cups green beans (1 green)
- 1 tsp olive oil (1/2 condiment)
- Pepper (1/4 condiment)
- Salt (1/4 condiment)

Directions:

1. In a bowl, toss green beans with oil. Season with pepper and salt.

2. Transfer green beans into the air fryer basket and cook at 390 F for 10 minutes.

3. Serve and enjoy.

Nutrition

- 27 Calories
- 1.2g Fat
- 1g Protein

Spicy Brussels Sprouts

Difficulty: Easy

Preparation Time: 10 minutes

Cooking Time: 14 minutes

Servings: 2

Ingredients:

- 1/2 lb. Brussels sprouts, trimmed and halved (1 lean)
- 1/2 tsp chili powder (1/4 condiment)
- 1/4 tsp cayenne (1/4 condiment)
- 1/2 tbsp olive oil (1/4 condiment)
- 1/4 tsp smoked paprika (1/4 condiment)

Directions:

1. Mix all ingredients into the large bowl and toss well.

2. Add Brussels sprouts into the air fryer basket and cook at 370 F for 14 minutes.

3. Serve and enjoy.

Nutrition

- 82 Calories
- 4g Fat
- 4g Protein

Delicious Ratatouille

Difficulty: Difficult

Preparation Time: 10 minutes

Cooking Time: 15 minutes

Servings: 6

Ingredients:

- 1 eggplant, diced (1/2 green)
- 3 garlic cloves, chopped (1/4 condiment)
- 1 onion, diced (1/4 condiment)
- 3 tomatoes, diced (1/2 healthy fat)
- 2 bell peppers, diced (1/2 green)
- 1 tbsp vinegar (1/4 condiment)
- 1 1/2 tbsp olive oil (1/4 condiment)
- 2 tbsp herb de Provence (1/2 green)
- Pepper (1/8 condiment)
- Salt (1/8 condiment)

Directions:

1. Preheat the air fryer to 400 F.

2. Add all ingredients into the bowl and toss well.

3. Add vegetable mixture into the air fryer basket and cook for 15 minutes. Stir halfway through.

4. Serve and enjoy.

Nutrition

- 83 Calories
- 4g Fat
- 2g Protein

Almond Flour Battered 'n Crisped Onion Rings

Difficulty: Average

Preparation Time: 10 minutes

Cooking Time: 15 minutes

Servings: 3

Ingredients:

- ½ cup almond flour (1/4 healthy fat)
- ¾ cup coconut milk (1/4 healthy fat)
- 1 big white onion, sliced into rings (1 green)
- 1 egg, beaten (1/4 healthy fat)
- 1 tablespoon baking powder (1/4 condiment)
- 1 tablespoon smoked paprika (1/4 condiment)
- Salt and pepper to taste (1/8 condiment)

Directions:

1. Preheat the air fryer for 5 minutes.

2. In a mixing bowl, mix the almond flour, baking powder, smoked paprika, salt and pepper.

3. In another bowl, combine the eggs and coconut milk.

4. Soak the onion slices into the egg mixture.

5. Dredge the onion slices in the almond flour mixture.

6. Place in the air fryer basket.

7. Close and cook for 15 minutes at 3250F.

8. Halfway through the cooking time, shake the fryer basket for even cooking.

Nutrition:

- 217 Calories
- 5.3g Protein
- 18g Fat

Spicy Asparagus Spears

Difficulty: Easy

Preparation Time: 10 minutes

Cooking Time: 15 minutes

Servings: 4

Ingredients:

- 35 asparagus spears, cut the ends (2 green)
- 1/2 tsp chili powder (1/4 condiment)
- 1/4 tsp paprika (1/4 condiment)
- 1 tbsp olive oil (1/4 condiment)
- Pepper (1/8 condiment)
- Salt (1/8 condiment)

Directions:

1. Add asparagus into the large bowl. Drizzle with oil.

2. Sprinkle with paprika, chili powder, pepper, and salt. Toss well.

3. Add asparagus into the air fryer basket and cook at 400 F for 15 minutes.

4. Serve and enjoy.

Nutrition

- 75 Calories
- 3.8g Fat
- 4.7g Protein

Healthy Asparagus Spears

Difficulty: Easy

Preparation Time: 10 minutes

Cooking Time: 15 minutes

Servings: 4

Ingredients:

- 35 asparagus spears, cut the ends (2 green)
- 1/2 tsp garlic powder (1/4 condiment)
- 1 tbsp olive oil (1/4 condiment)
- Pepper (1/8 condiment)
- Salt (1/8 condiment)
- ¼ tsp. onion powder (1/4 condiment)

Directions:

1. Add asparagus into the large bowl. Drizzle with oil.

2. Sprinkle with onion powder, garlic powder, pepper, and salt. Toss well.

3. Arrange asparagus into the air fryer basket and cook at 375 F for 15 minutes.

4. Serve and enjoy.

Nutrition

- 75 Calories
- 4g Fat
- 4g Protein

Mediterranean-Style Eggs with Spinach

Difficulty: Easy

Preparation Time: 3 minutes

Cooking Time: 12 minutes

Servings: 2

Ingredients:

- 2 tablespoons olive oil, melted (1/4 condiment)
- 4 eggs, whisked (1 healthy fat)
- 5 ounces' fresh spinach, chopped (1 green)
- 1 medium-sized tomato, chopped (1 green)
- 1 teaspoon fresh lemon juice (1/4 condiment)
- 1/2 teaspoon coarse salt (1/8 condiment)
- 1/2 teaspoon ground black pepper (1/8 condiment)
- 1/2 cup of fresh basil, roughly chopped (1/4 green)

Directions:

1. Add the olive oil to an Air Fryer baking pan. Make sure to tilt the pan to spread the oil evenly.

2. Simply combine the remaining ingredients, except for the basil leaves; whisk well until everything is well incorporated.

3. Cook in the preheated oven for 8 to 12 minutes at 280 degrees F. Garnish with fresh basil leaves. Serve.

Nutrition:

- 274 Calories
- 23g Fat
- 14g Protein

Creamy Cauliflower and Broccoli

Difficulty: Average

Preparation Time: 4 minutes

Cooking Time: 16 minutes

Servings: 6

Ingredients:

- 1-pound cauliflower florets (1 green)
- 1-pound broccoli florets (1 green)
- 2 ½ tablespoons sesame oil (1/2 condiment)
- 1/2 teaspoon smoked cayenne pepper (1/4 condiment)
- 3/4 teaspoon sea salt flakes (1/4 condiment)
- 1 tablespoon lemon zest, grated (1/4 condiment)
- 1/2 cup Colby cheese, shredded (1/2 healthy fat)

Directions:

1. Prepare the cauliflower and broccoli using your favorite steaming method. Then, drain

them well; add the sesame oil, cayenne pepper, and salt flakes.

2. Air-fry at 390 degrees F for approximately 16 minutes; make sure to check the vegetables halfway through the cooking time.

3. Afterward, stir in the lemon zest and Colby cheese; toss to coat well and serve immediately!

Nutrition:

- 133 Calories
- 9g Fat
- 6g Protein

Fried Squash Croquettes

Difficulty: Easy

Preparation Time: 5 minutes

Cooking Time: 17 minutes

Servings: 4

Ingredients:

- 1/3 cup all-purpose flour (1/4 condiment)
- 1/3 teaspoon freshly ground black pepper, or more to taste (1/4 condiment)
- 1/3 teaspoon dried sage (1/8 condiment)
- 4 cloves garlic, minced (1/4 condiment)
- 1 ½ tablespoons olive oil (1/4 condiment)
- 1/3 butternut squash, peeled and grated
- 2 eggs, well whisked (1 healthy fat)
- 1 teaspoon fine sea salt (1/8 condiment)
- A pinch of ground allspice (1/8 condiment)

Directions:

1. Thoroughly combine all ingredients in a mixing bowl.

2. Preheat your Air Fryer to 345 degrees and set the timer for 17 minutes; cook until your fritters are browned; serve right away.

Nutrition:

- 152 Calories
- 10g Fat
- 6g Protein

Cheese Stuffed Mushrooms with Horseradish Sauce

Difficulty: Average

Preparation Time: 3 minutes

Cooking Time: 12 minutes

Servings: 5

Ingredients:

- 1/2 cup parmesan cheese, grated (1/4 healthy fat)
- 2 cloves garlic, pressed (1/4 condiment)
- 2 tablespoons fresh coriander, chopped (1/4 green)
- 1/3 teaspoon kosher salt (1/8 condiment)
- 1/2 teaspoon crushed red pepper flakes (1/8 condiment)
- 1 ½ tablespoons olive oil (1/4 condiment)
- 20 medium-sized mushrooms, cut off the stems (1 healthy fat)
- 1/2 cup Gorgonzola cheese, grated (1/2 healthy fat)
- 1/4 cup low-fat mayonnaise (1/4 healthy fat)
- 1 teaspoon prepared horseradish, well-drained (1/4 green)
- 1 tablespoon fresh parsley, finely chopped (1/4 green)

Directions:

1. Mix the parmesan cheese together with the garlic, coriander, salt, red pepper, and olive oil; mix to combine well.

2. Stuff the mushroom caps with the cheese filling. Top with grated Gorgonzola.

3. Place the mushrooms in the Air Fryer grill pan and slide them into the machine. Grill them at 380 degrees F for 8 to 12 minutes or until the stuffing is warmed through.

4. Meanwhile, prepare the horseradish sauce by mixing the mayonnaise, horseradish and parsley. Serve the horseradish sauce with the warm fried mushrooms. Enjoy!

Nutrition:

- 180 Calories
- 13.2g Fat
- 9g Protein

Air Fryer Bell Peppers

Difficulty: Easy

Preparation Time: 10 minutes

Cooking Time: 8 minutes

Servings: 3

Ingredients:

- ¼ tsp. onion powder (1/4 condiment)
- 3 cups bell peppers, cut into pieces (1 green)
- 1 tsp olive oil (1/2 condiment)
- 1/4 tsp garlic powder (1/4 condiment)

Directions:

1. Mix all ingredients into the large bowl and toss well.
2. Transfer bell peppers into the air fryer basket and cook at 360 F for 8 minutes. Stir halfway through.
3. Serve and enjoy.

Nutrition

- 52 Calories
- 2g Fat
- 1.2g Protein

Broccoli with Herbs and Cheese

Difficulty: Average

Preparation Time: 8 minutes

Cooking Time: 17 minutes

Servings: 4

Ingredients:

- 1/3 cup grated yellow cheese (1/2 healthy fat)
- 1 large-sized head broccoli, stemmed and cut small florets (1 green)
- 2 1/2 tablespoons canola oil (1/8 condiment)
- 2 teaspoons dried rosemary (1/4 green)
- 2 teaspoons dried basil (1/4 green)
- Salt and ground black pepper to taste (1/8 condiment)

Directions:

1. Bring a medium pan filled with a lightly salted water to a boil. Then, boil the broccoli florets for about 3 minutes.
2. Then, drain the broccoli florets well; toss them with canola oil, rosemary, basil, salt and black pepper.
3. Set your oven to 390 degrees F; arrange the seasoned broccoli in the cooking basket; set the timer for 17 minutes. Toss the broccoli halfway through the cooking process.
4. Serve warm topped with grated cheese and enjoy!

Nutrition:

- 111 Calories
- 2.1g Fat
- 8.9g Protein

Cheese Broccoli Fritters

Difficulty: Average

Preparation Time: 10 minutes

Cooking Time: 30 minutes

Servings: 4

Ingredients:

- 2 eggs, lightly beaten (1/2 healthy fat)
- 3 cups broccoli florets, cook & mashed (1 lean)
- 2 cups cheddar cheese (1/2 healthy fat)
- 1/4 cup almond flour (1/4 condiment)
- 2 garlic cloves, minced (1/4 condiment)
- Pepper (1/4 condiment)
- Salt (1/4 condiment)

Directions:

1. Mix all ingredients into the bowl.
2. Make patties from mixture and place them into the basket and cook at 350 F for 15 minutes.
3. Turn patties and cook for 15 minutes more.
4. Serve and enjoy.

Nutrition

- 285 Calories
- 21g Fat
- 18g Protein

Healthy & Tasty Green Beans

Difficulty: Easy

Preparation Time: 10 minutes

Cooking Time: 10 minutes

Servings: 2

Ingredients:

- 2 cups green beans (1/2 green)
- 1/8 tsp ground allspice (1/8 condiment)
- 1/4 tsp ground cinnamon (1/8 condiment)
- 1/2 tsp dried oregano (1/4 green)
- 2 tbsp olive oil (1/8 condiment)
- 1/4 tsp ground coriander (1/8 condiment)
- 1/4 tsp ground cumin (1/8 condiment)
- 1/8 tsp cayenne pepper (1/8 condiment)
- 1/2 tsp salt (1/8 condiment)

Directions:

1. Add all ingredients into the bowl and toss well.

2. Add green beans into the air fryer basket and cook at 370 F for 10 minutes. Shake basket halfway through

3. Serve and enjoy.

Nutrition

- 158 Calories
- 14g Fat
- 2.1g Protein

Spanish-Style Eggs with Manchego Cheese

Difficulty: Difficult
Preparation Time: 10 minutes
Cooking Time: 38 minutes
Servings: 4
Ingredients:

- 1/3 cup grated Manchego cheese (1/2 healthy fat)
- 5 eggs (2 healthy fats)
- 2 green garlic stalks, peeled and finely minced (1 green)
- 1 ½ cups white mushrooms, chopped (1 healthy fat)
- 1 teaspoon dried basil (1/4 green)
- 1 ½ tablespoons olive oil (1/2 condiment)
- 3/4 teaspoon dried oregano (1/4 green)
- 1/2 teaspoon dried parsley flakes or 1 tablespoon fresh flat-leaf Italian parsley (1/4 green)
- 1 teaspoon porcini powder (1/8 condiment)

- Table salt and freshly ground black pepper to taste (1/8 condiment)

Directions:

1. Start by preheating your Air Fryer to 350 degrees F. Add the oil, mushrooms, and green garlic to the Air Fryer baking dish. Bake this mixture for 6 minutes or until it is tender.

2. Meanwhile, crack the eggs into a mixing bowl; beat the eggs until they're well whisked. Next, add the seasonings and mix again. Pause your Air Fryer and take the baking dish out of the basket.

3. Pour the whisked egg mixture into the baking dish with sautéed mixture. Top with the grated Manchego cheese.

4. Bake for about 32 minutes at 320 degrees F or until your frittata is set. Serve warm. Bon appétit!

Nutrition:

- 153 Calories
- 12g Fat
- 9g Protein

Air Fryer Broccoli & Brussels Sprouts

Difficulty: Average
Preparation Time: 10 minutes
Cooking Time: 30 minutes
Servings: 6
Ingredients:

- 1 lb. Brussels sprouts, cut ends (1 green)
- 1 lb. broccoli, cut into florets (1 green)
- 1 tsp paprika (1/4 condiment)
- 1 tsp garlic powder (1/4 condiment)
- 1/2 tsp pepper (1/4 condiment)
- 3 tbsp olive oil (1 healthy fat)
- 3/4 tsp salt (1/4 condiment)

Directions:

1. Add all ingredients into the bowl and toss well.

2. Add vegetable mixture into the air fryer basket and cook at 370 F for 30 minutes.

3. Serve and enjoy.

Nutrition

- 125 Calories

- 7.6g Fat
- 5g Protein

Creamy Spinach and Mushroom Lasagna

Difficulty: Easy

Preparation Time: 60 minutes

Cooking Time: 20 minutes

Servings: 6

Ingredients:

- 10 lasagna noodles (2 healthy fat)
- 1 package whole milk ricotta (1 healthy fat)
- 2 packages of frozen chopped spinach. (2 green)
- 4 cups mozzarella cheese (divided and shredded) (1 healthy fat)
- 3/4 cup grated fresh Parmesan (1/2 healthy fat)
- 3 tablespoons chopped fresh parsley leaves(optional) (1/4 green)

For the Sauce:

- 1/4 cup butter(unsalted) (1/4 healthy fat)
- 2 cloves garlic (1/8 condiment)
- 1 pound of thinly sliced cremini mushroom (1/4 healthy fat)
- 1 diced onion (1/8 condiment)
- 1/4 cup flour (1/4 condiment)
- 4 cups milk, kept at room temperature (1 healthy fat)
- 1 teaspoon basil(dried) (1/8 green)
- Pinch of nutmeg (1/8 condiment)

Directions:

1. Preheat oven to 352 degrees F.

2. To make the sauce, over a medium portion of heat, melt your butter, add garlic, mushrooms and onion. Cook and stir at intervals until it becomes tender at about 3-4 minutes.

3. Whisk in flour until lightly browned, it takes about 1 minute for it to become brown.

4. Next, whisk in the milk gradually, and cook, whisking always, about 2-3 minute till it becomes thickened. Stir in basil, oregano and nutmeg, season with salt and pepper for taste;

5. Then set aside.

6. In another pot of boiling salted water, cook lasagna noodles according to the package instructions.

7. Spread 1 cup mushroom sauce onto the bottom of a baking dish; top it with 4 lasagna noodles, 1/2 of the spinach, 1 cup mozzarella cheese and 1/4 cup Parmesan.

8. Repeat this process with remaining noodles, mushroom sauce, and cheeses.

9. Place into the oven and bake for 35-45 minutes, or until it starts bubbling. Then boil for 2-3 minutes until it becomes brown and translucent.

10. Let cool for 15 minutes.

11. Serve it with garnished parsley (Optional)

Nutrition:

- 488 Calories
- 19g Fats
- 25g Protein

Stuffed Mushrooms

Difficulty: Average

Preparation Time: 10 minutes

Cooking Time: 8 minutes

Servings: 16

Ingredients:

- 16 mushrooms, clean and chop stems (3 healthy fats)
- 2 garlic cloves, minced (1/2 condiment)
- 1/2 tsp chili powder (1/4 condiment)
- 1/4 cup cheddar cheese, shredded (1/2 healthy fat)
- 2 oz crab meat, chopped (1 lean)
- 8 oz cream cheese, softened (1/2 healthy fat)
- 1/4 tsp pepper (1/4 condiment)

Directions:

1. In a bowl, mix cheese, mushroom stems, chili powder, pepper, crabmeat, cream cheese, and garlic until well combined.

2. Stuff mushrooms with cheese mixture and place them into the air fryer basket and cook at 370 F for 8 minutes.

3. Serve and enjoy.

Nutrition

- 65 Calories

- 5.3g Fat
- 2.6g Protein

Family Favorite Stuffed Mushrooms

Difficulty: Easy

Preparation Time:4 minutes

Cooking Time: 12 minutes

Servings: 2

Ingredients:

- 2 teaspoons cumin powder (1/4 condiment)
- 4 garlic cloves, peeled and minced (1/4 condiment)
- 18 medium-sized white mushrooms (2 healthy fats)
- Fine sea salt and freshly ground black pepper to taste (1/8 condiment)
- A pinch ground allspice (1/8 condiment)
- 2 tablespoons olive oil (1/4 condiment)

Directions:

1. First, clean the mushrooms; remove the middle stalks from the mushrooms to prepare the "shells."

2. Grab a mixing dish and thoroughly combine the remaining items. Fill the mushrooms with the prepared mixture.

3. Cook the mushrooms at 345 degrees F heat for 12 minutes. Enjoy!

Nutrition:

- 179 Calories
- 15g Fat
- 6g Protein

Thai Roasted Veggies

Difficulty: Easy

Preparation Time: 20 minutes

Cooking Time: 6 to 8 hours

Servings: 8

Ingredients:

- 4 large carrots, peeled and cut into chunks (2 green)
- 6 garlic cloves, peeled and sliced (1/4 condiment)
- 2 parsnips, peeled and sliced (1/2 green)
- 2 jalapeño peppers, minced (1/2 green)
- 1/2 cup Roasted Vegetable Broth (1 condiment)
- 1/3 cup canned coconut milk (1/2 healthy fat)
- 3 tablespoons lime juice (1/8 condiment)
- 2 tablespoons grated fresh ginger root (1/4 condiment)
- 2 teaspoons curry powder (1/8 condiment)

Directions:

1. In a 6-quart slow cooker, mix the carrots, garlic, parsnips, and jalapeño peppers.

2. In a small bowl, mix the vegetable broth, coconut milk, lime juice, ginger root, and curry powder until well blended. Pour this mixture into the slow cooker.

3. Cover and cook on low for 6 to 8 hours, do it until the vegetables are tender when pierced with a fork.

Nutrition:

- 69 Calories
- 3g Fat
- 1g Protein

Famous Fried Pickles

Difficulty: Average

Preparation Time: 5 minutes

Cooking Time: 15 minutes

Servings: 6

Ingredients:

- 1/3 cup milk (1/2 healthy fat)
- 1 teaspoon garlic powder (1/8 condiment)
- 2 medium-sized eggs (1 healthy fat)
- 1 teaspoon fine sea salt (1/8 condiment)
- 1/3 teaspoon chili powder (1/4 condiment)
- 1/3 cup all-purpose flour (1/4 healthy fat)
- 1/2 teaspoon shallot powder (1/4 condiment)
- 2 jars sweet and sour pickle spears (1 healthy fat)

Directions:

1. Pat the pickle spears dry with a kitchen towel. Then take two mixing bowls.

2. Whisk the egg and milk in a bowl. In another bowl, combine all dry ingredients.

3. Firstly, dip the pickle spears into the dry mix; then coat each pickle with the egg/milk mixture; dredge them in the flour mixture again for additional coating.

4. Air fry battered pickles for 15 minutes at 385 degrees. Enjoy!

Nutrition:

- 58 Calories
- 2g Fat
- 3.2g Protein

Kale Slaw and Strawberry Salad + Poppyseed Dressing

Difficulty: Easy

Preparation Time: 10 minutes

Cooking Time: 20 minutes

Servings: 2

Ingredients:

- Chicken breast; 8 ounces; sliced and baked (2 lean)
- Kale; 1 cup; chopped (1/4 green)
- Slaw mix; 1 cup (cabbage, broccoli slaw, carrots mixed) (1 green)
- Slivered almonds; 1/4 cup (1/4 healthy fat)
- Strawberries; 1 cup; sliced (1/4 healthy fat)

For the dressing:

- Light mayonnaise; 1 tablespoon (1/8 healthy fat)
- Dijon mustard (1/8 condiment)
- Olive oil; 1 tablespoon (1/8 condiment)
- Apple cider vinegar; 1 tablespoon (1/8 condiment)
- Lemon juice; 1/2 teaspoon (1/8 condiment)
- 1 tablespoon of Honey (1/8 condiment)
- Onion powder; 1/4 teaspoon (1/8 condiment)
- Garlic powder; 1/4 teaspoon (1/8 condiment)
- Poppyseeds (1/8 healthy fat)

Directions:

1. Whisk the dressing ingredients together until well mixed, then leave to cool in the fridge.

2. Slice the chicken breasts.

3. Divide 2 bowls of spinach, slaw, and strawberries.

4. Cover with a sliced breast of chicken (4 oz. each), then scatter with almonds.

5. Divide the salad over the dressing and drizzle.

Nutrition:

- 340 Calories
- 14g Fats
- 6.2 g Protein

Asian Stir Fry

Difficulty: Easy

Preparation Time: 15 minutes

Cooking Time: 10 minutes

Servings: 4

Ingredients:

- 1 tsp. Olive oil (1/8 condiment)
- 1 Tsp. Low Soy Sodium Sauce (1/8 condiment)
- 1 Lime Wedge (1/8 Lime) (1/8 condiment)
- Split into strips 7 ounces of boneless, skinless chicken breast (2 lean)
- C 3/4 Broccoli blossoms (1 green)
- 1/2 C. Sliced Chestnuts (1/2 healthy fat)
- 1/4 hp. Red bell pepper split (1/4 green)
- 1/4 hp. Freshwater (1/8 condiment)
- New ground potatoes, to taste (1/4 condiment)

Directions:

1. Prepare meat and veggies.

2. Add oil, soy sauce and lime wedge juice in a medium to large skillet.

3. Put on medium heat, then add chicken. Cook chicken over regularly, tossing or stirring.

4. Remove the chicken from the saucepan and put it aside.

5. Add water to the saucepan and stir until the water gets warm.

6. Next, add the vegetables and mix well to ensure that they are all eaten.

7. Cover and let cook for 5-7 minutes until almost tender vegetables.

8. Remove the cover and add the chicken, cook over medium-high to high heat until the vegetables are cooked, and the liquid is evaporated completely

Nutrition:
- 13g Carbohydrates
- 4g Protein
- 8g Fat

Cheesy Broccoli Cauliflower

Difficulty: Easy
Preparation Time: 10 minutes
Cooking Time: 20 minutes
Servings: 6
Ingredients:

- 4 cups cauliflower florets (1 green)
- 4 cups broccoli florets (1 green)
- 2/3 cup parmesan cheese, shredded (1 healthy fat)
- 5 garlic cloves, minced (1/2 condiment)
- 1/3 cup olive oil (1/4 condiment)
- Pepper (1/8 condiment)
- Salt (1/8 condiment)

Directions:

1. Add half cheese, broccoli, cauliflower, garlic, oil, pepper, and salt into the bowl and toss well.
2. Add broccoli and cauliflower to the air fryer basket and cook at 370 F for 20 minutes.
3. Add remaining cheese. Toss well.
4. Serve and enjoy.

Nutrition
- 165 Calories
- 13.6g Fat
- 6.4g Protein

Roasted Squash Puree

Difficulty: Easy
Preparation Time: 20 minutes
Cooking Time: 6 to 7 hours
Servings: 8
Ingredients:

- 1 (3-pound) butternut squash, peeled, seeded, and cut into 1-inch pieces (1 green)
- 3 (1-pound) acorn squash, peeled, seeded, and cut into 1-inch pieces (2 green)
- 3 garlic cloves, minced (1/4 condiment)
- 2 tablespoons olive oil (1/8 condiment)
- 1 teaspoon dried marjoram leaves (1/8 green)
- 1/2 teaspoon salt (1/8 condiment)
- 1/8 teaspoon freshly ground black pepper (1/8 condiment)

Directions:

1. In a 6-quart slow cooker, mix all of the ingredients.
2. Cover and cook on low for 6 to 7 hours, or until the squash is tender when pierced with a fork.
3. Use a potato masher to mash the squash right in the slow cooker.

Nutrition:
- 175 Calories
- 4g Fat
- 3g Protein

Cauliflower Crust Pizza

Difficulty: Average
Preparation Time: 20 minutes
Cooking Time: 45 minutes
Servings: 4
Ingredients:

- 1 cauliflower (1 green)
- 1/4 grated parmesan cheese (1/2 healthy fat)
- 1 egg (1/4 healthy fat)
- 1Tsp Italian seasoning (1/8 condiment)
- 1/4 Tsp. kosher salt (1/8 condiment)
- 2 cups of freshly grated mozzarella (1/4 healthy fat)
- 1/4 cup of spicy pizza sauce (1/8 condiment)
- Basil leaves for garnishing (1/4 green)

Directions:

1. Begin by preheating your oven while using the parchment paper to rim the baking sheet.
2. Process the cauliflower into a fine powder, and then transfer to a bowl before putting it into the microwave.
3. Leave for about 5-6 minutes to get it soft.
4. Transfer the microwave cauliflower to a clean and dry kitchen towel.
5. Leave it to cool off.

6. When cold, use the kitchen towel to wrap the cauliflower and then get rid of all the moisture by wringing the towel.

7. Continue squeezing until the water is gone completely.

8. Put the cauliflower, Italian seasoning, Parmesan, egg, salt, and mozzarella (1 cup).

9. Stir very well until well combined.

10. Transfer the combined mixture to the baking sheet previously prepared, pressing it into a 10-inch round shape.

11. Bake for 10-15 minutes until it becomes golden in color.

12. Take the baked crust out of the oven and use the spicy pizza sauce and mozzarella (the leftover 1 cup) to top it.

13. Bake again for 10 more minutes until the cheese melts and looks bubbly.

14. Garnish using fresh basil leaves.

15. You can also enjoy this with salad.

Nutrition:
- 74 Calories
- 6g Protein
- 4g Fat

Spicy Zesty Broccoli with Tomato Sauce

Difficulty: Average

Preparation Time: 5 minutes

Cooking Time: 15 minutes

Servings: 6

Ingredients:

For the Broccoli Bites:

- 1 medium-sized head broccoli, broken into florets (1 green)
- 1/2 teaspoon lemon zest, freshly grated (1/4 condiment)
- 1/3 teaspoon fine sea salt (1/8 condiment)
- 1/2 teaspoon hot paprika (1/8 condiment)
- 1 teaspoon shallot powder (1/8 condiment)
- 1 teaspoon porcini powder (1/8 condiment)
- 1/2 teaspoon granulated garlic (1/8 condiment)
- 1/3 teaspoon celery seeds (1/4 healthy fat)
- 1 ½ tablespoons olive oil (1/8 condiment)

For the Hot Sauce:

- 1/2 cup tomato sauce (1/2 healthy fat)
- 1 tablespoon balsamic vinegar (1/8 condiment)
- ½ teaspoon ground allspice (1/8 condiment)

Directions:

1. Toss all the ingredients for the broccoli bites in a mixing bowl, covering the broccoli florets on all sides.

2. Cook them in the preheated Air Fryer at 360 degrees for 13 to 15 minutes. In the meantime, mix all ingredients for the hot sauce.

3. Pause your Air Fryer, mix the broccoli with the prepared sauce and cook for a further 3 minutes. Bon appétit!

Nutrition:
- 70 Calories
- 4g Fat
- 2g Protein

Tamarind Glazed Sweet Potatoes

Difficulty: Easy

Preparation Time: 2 minutes

Cooking Time: 22 minutes

Servings: 4

Ingredients:

- 1/3 teaspoon white pepper (1/8 condiment)
- 1 tablespoon butter, melted (1/4 healthy fat)
- 1/2 teaspoon turmeric powder (1/8 condiment)
- 5 garnet sweet potatoes, peeled and diced (2 healthy fat)
- A few drops liquid Stevia (1/8 condiment)
- 2 teaspoons tamarind paste (1/4 condiment)
- 1 1/2 tablespoons fresh lime juice (1/8 condiment)
- 1 1/2 teaspoon ground allspice (1/8 condiment)

Directions:

1. In a mixing bowl, toss all ingredients until sweet potatoes are well coated.

2. Air-fry them at 335 degrees F for 12 minutes.

3. Pause the Air Fryer and toss again. Increase the temperature to 390 degrees F and cook for an additional 10 minutes. Eat warm.

Nutrition:

- 103 Calories
- 9g Fat
- 1.9g Protein

Simple Green Beans with Butter

Difficulty: Easy

Preparation Time: 2 minutes

Cooking Time: 10 minutes

Servings: 4

Ingredients:

- 3/4-pound green beans, cleaned
- 1 tablespoon balsamic vinegar
- 1/4 teaspoon kosher salt
- 1/2 teaspoon mixed peppercorns, freshly cracked
- 1 tablespoon butter
- 2 tablespoons toasted sesame seeds to serve

Directions:

1. Set your Air Fryer to cook at 390 degrees F.

2. Mix the green beans with all of the above ingredients, apart from the sesame seeds. Set the timer for 10 minutes.

3. Meanwhile, toast the sesame seeds in a small-sized nonstick skillet; make sure to stir continuously.

4. Serve sautéed green beans on a nice serving platter sprinkled with toasted sesame seeds. Bon appétit!

Nutrition:

- 73 Calories
- 3g Fat
- 1.6g Protein

Roasted Cauliflower with Pepper Jack Cheese

Difficulty: Average

Preparation Time: 4 minutes

Cooking Time: 21 minutes

Servings: 2

Ingredients:

- 1/3 teaspoon shallot powder (1/4 condiment)
- 1 teaspoon ground black pepper (1/8 condiment)
- 1 ½ large-sized heads of cauliflower, broken into florets (1 green)
- 1/4 teaspoon cumin powder (1/8 condiment)
- ½ teaspoon garlic salt (1/8 condiment)
- 1/4 cup Pepper Jack cheese, grated (1/4 healthy fat)
- 1 ½ tablespoons vegetable oil (1/8 condiment)
- 1/3 teaspoon paprika (1/8 condiment)

Directions:

1. Boil cauliflower in a large pan of salted water for approximately 5 minutes. After that, drain the cauliflower florets; now transfer them to a baking dish.

2. Toss the cauliflower florets with the rest of the above ingredients.

3. Roast at 395 degrees F for 16 minutes, turn them halfway through the process. Enjoy!

Nutrition:

- 271 Calories
- 23g Fat
- Protein

Tomato Bites with Creamy Parmesan Sauce

Difficulty: Easy

Preparation Time:7 minutes

Cooking Time: 13 minutes

Servings: 4

Ingredients:

For the Sauce:

- 1/2 cup Parmigiano-Reggiano cheese, grated (1/4 healthy fat)
- 4 tablespoons pecans, chopped (1/2 healthy fat)
- 1 teaspoon garlic puree (1/8 condiment)
- 1/2 teaspoon fine sea salt (1/8 condiment)
- 1/3 cup extra-virgin olive oil (1/8 condiment)

For the Tomato Bites:

- 2 large-sized Roma tomatoes, cut into thin slices and pat them dry (1 green)
- 8 ounces Halloumi cheese, cut into thin slices (1 healthy fat)
- 1 teaspoon dried basil (1/2 green)
- 1/4 teaspoon red pepper flakes, crushed (1/8 condiment)
- 1/8 teaspoon sea salt (1/8 condiment)

Directions:

1. Start by preheating your Air Fryer to 385 degrees F.

2. Make the sauce by mixing all ingredients, except the extra-virgin olive oil, in your food processor.

3. While the machine is running, slowly and gradually pour in the olive oil; puree until everything is well - blended.

4. Now, spread 1 teaspoon of the sauce over the top of each tomato slice. Place a slice of Halloumi cheese on each tomato slice. Top with onion slices. Sprinkle with basil, red pepper, and sea salt.

5. Transfer the assembled bites to the Air Fryer. Spray with non-stick cooking spray and cook for about 13 minutes.

6. Arrange these bites on a nice serving platter, garnish with the remaining sauce, and serve at room temperature. Bon appétit!

Nutrition:

- 428 Calories
- 38g Fat
- 18g Protein

Salad Recipes

Chicken Salad with Pineapple and Pecans

Difficulty: Average
Preparation Time: 13 minutes
Cooking Time: 9 minutes
Servings: 4
Ingredients

- 6-ounce boneless, skinless, cooked and cubed chicken breast (2 lean)
- Tablespoons of celery hacked (1/2 green)
- ¼ cup of cut pineapple (1/4 healthy fat)
- ¼ cup orange peeled segments (1/4 healthy fat)
- Tablespoon of pecans hacked (1/4 healthy fat)
- ¼ cup seedless grapes (1/4 healthy fat)
- Salt and black chili pepper, to taste (1/4 condiment)
- 3 Cups of cut romaine lettuce (1 green)

Directions:

1. Put chicken, celery, pineapple, grapes, pecans, and raisins in a medium dish. Kindly blend until mixed with a spoon, then season with salt and pepper.

2. Create a bed of lettuce on a plate. Cover with mixture of chicken and serve.

Nutrition

- 391 calories
- 37g fat
- 21g protein

Santa Fe Taco Salad

Difficulty: Average
Preparation Time: 11 minutes
Cooking Time: 16 minutes
Servings: 3
Ingredients
Toppings:

- ½ pound 93 percent lean ground turkey (1 lean)

- 1/2 cup dried, rinsed, and drained black beans (1/2 healthy fat)
- Seasoned jalapeño chili pepper (1/4 green)
- Beefsteak tomatoes, chopped (1/2 healthy fat)
- 1 Clove of garlic, minced and peeled (1/8 condiment)
- 3 tablespoons of chopped scallions (1/2 green)
- 2 tablespoons of fresh cilantro chopped, plus garnish (1/2 green)
- Salt and ground black pepper, sweet paprika to taste 1 ¼ teaspoon (1/8 condiment)

For the Avocado Dip:

- ¼ cup, 2% Greek yogurt (1/2 healthy fat)
- ¼ cup of water (1/2 condiment)
- 1 medium avocado, peeled, pitted, chopped, and split (1/2 healthy fat)
- 1 ½ spoonful of fresh cilantro (1/4 green)
- ½ tablespoon cayenne pepper (1/8 condiment)
- Salt and black chili pepper, to taste (1/8 condiment)

For the Salad:

- 5 cups shredded iceberg lettuce cup shredded (1 green)
- 1 Mexican cheese mixed beefsteak tomato, chopped (1/2 healthy fat)
- Tablespoons of fresh coriander (1/2 green)
- 2 spoons smashed tortilla chips (1/2 healthy fat)

Directions:

1. Heat a broad skillet over medium-high heat, without sticking. Use a wooden spoon to split the meat into small pieces and add the ground turkey to the skillet. Cook, stirring constantly, for 4 to 5 minutes until the meat is no longer pink.

2. Incorporate beans, jalapeño, onions, garlic, scallions, salt, pepper, and paprika. Reduce heat to low, cover, and cook for 15 minutes. Remove the lid from the skillet and cook for about 5 minutes until the liquid decreases.

3. In the meantime, make the avocado dip: add yogurt, sugar, half the avocado, cilantro, cayenne, salt, and pepper into a blender. Up to a smooth process; reserve.

4. Divide the lettuce into 4 slabs. Top with the mixture of beef, cheese, onions, cilantro, and chopped avocado left over. Add the avocado dip over the top and garnish the chips with crushed tortilla.

Nutrition

- 491 calories
- 28g fat
- 11g protein

Coleslaw Worth A Second Helping

Difficulty: Easy

Preparation Time: 20 minutes

Cooking Time: 10 minutes

Servings: 6

Ingredients:

- 5 cups shredded cabbage (2 green)
- 2 carrots, shredded (1 green)
- ½ cup mayonnaise (1/2 healthy fat)
- ½ cup sour cream (1/2 healthy fat)
- 3 tablespoons apple cider vinegar (1/2 condiment)
- 1 teaspoon kosher salt (1/4 condiment)
- ½ teaspoon celery seed (1/4 condiment)

Directions:

1. Add together the cabbage, carrots, and parsley in a large bowl.

2. Whisk together the mayonnaise, sour cream, vinegar, salt, and celery in a small bowl until smooth. Pour sauce over veggies and pour until covered. Transfer to a serving bowl and bake until ready to serve.

Nutrition:

- 192 Calories
- 18g Total fat
- 2g Protein

Grilled Mediterranean Salad

Difficulty: Average

Preparation Time: 10 minutes

Cooking Time: 8 minutes

Servings: 3

Ingredients:

- ¼ cup balsamic vinegar (1/8 condiment)
- ½ teaspoon capers (1/8 condiment)
- ½ cup of coarse garlic (1/8 condiment)
- 2 tablespoons of dry-packed sun-dried tomatoes, roughly cut (1 healthy fat)
- 2 red bell peppers, sliced into large strips and seeded (1 healthy fat)
- 8 spikes of asparagus (2 green)
- Sliced zucchini (1 green)
- Teaspoons extra virgin olive oil (1/8 condiment)
- Salt and black chili pepper, to taste (1/8 condiment)
- 4 hard-boiled eggs, quartered and peeled (1 healthy fat)
- 2 tablespoons of Kalamata olives, finely chopped (1 healthy fat)
- ¼ cup crumbled feta cheese (1 healthy fat)
- Cut fresh basil to taste (1/8 green)

Directions:

1. Put the vinegar, capers, garlic, and sun-dried tomatoes into a food processor's cup. Method until well-knitted.

2. Combine the red peppers, asparagus, and zucchini in a large mixing bowl. Add extra virgin olive oil, salt, and pepper. Toss to merge.

3. Prepare a medium-high fire to barbecue. Cover the barbecue grills loosely with a cooking spray. Once the grill is hot, grill the vegetables until lightly charred, turning occasionally.

4. Add grilled veggies and vinaigrette in a bowl, and toss to combine. Divide the vegetables into four plates. Garnish with eggs, olives, feta, and basil.

Nutrition:

- 388 calories
- 34g fat
- 21g protein

Tomato Salsa

Difficulty: Easy

Preparation Time: 5 minutes

Cooking Time: 0 minutes

Servings: 6

Ingredients:

- 1 garlic clove, minced (1/4 condiment)
- 4 tablespoons olive oil (1/4 condiment)
- 5 tomatoes, cubed (1 healthy fat)
- 1 tablespoon balsamic vinegar (1/8 condiment)
- ¼ cup basil, chopped (1/4 green)
- 1 tablespoon parsley, chopped (1/4 green)
- 1 tablespoon chives, chopped (1/4 green)
- Salt and black pepper to the taste (1/8 condiment)
- Pita chips for serving (1 healthy fat)

Directions:

1. Mix the tomatoes with the garlic in a bowl, and the rest of the ingredients except the pita chips, stir, divide into small cups and serve with the pita chips on the side.

Nutrition:

- 160 Calories
- 14g Fat
- 2.2g Protein

Greek Salad

Difficulty: Easy

Preparation Time: 15 minutes

Cooking Time: 15 minutes

Servings: 5

Ingredients:

For Dressing:

- ½ teaspoon black pepper (1/8 condiment)
- ¼ teaspoon salt (1/8 condiment)
- ½ teaspoon oregano (1/8 green)
- 1 tablespoon garlic powder (1/8 condiment)
- 2 tablespoons Balsamic (1/8 condiment)
- 1/3 cup olive oil (1/8 condiment)

For Salad:

- ½ cup sliced black olives (1/4 healthy fat)
- ½ cup chopped parsley, fresh (1/4 green)

- 1 small red onion, thin-sliced (1/4 healthy fat)
- 1 cup cherry tomatoes, sliced (1/4 healthy fat)
- 1 bell pepper, yellow, chunked (1/4 green)
- 1 cucumber, peeled, quarter and slice (1/4 green)
- 4 cups chopped romaine lettuce (1 green)
- ½ teaspoon salt (1/8 condiment)
- 2 tablespoons olive oil (1/8 condiment)

Directions:

1. In a small container, join all of the ingredients for the dressing and let this set in the freezer while you make the salad.

2. To assemble the salad, mix together all the ingredients in a large-sized bowl and toss the veggies gently but thoroughly to mix.

3. Serve the salad with the dressing in amounts as desired

Nutrition:

- 234 Calories:
- 16g Fat
- 5g Protein

Grilled Mahi-Mahi with Jicama Slaw

Difficulty: Average

Preparation Time: 20 minutes

Cooking Time: 10 minutes

Servings: 4

Ingredients:

- 1 teaspoon each for pepper and salt, divided (1/8 condiment)
- 1 tablespoon of lime juice, divided (1/8 condiment)
- 2 tablespoon + 2 teaspoons of extra virgin olive oil (1/4 condiment)
- 4 raw mahi-mahi fillets, which should be about 8 oz. each (2 lean)
- ½ cucumber (1/2 green)
- 1 jicama (1/4 condiment)
- 1 cup of alfalfa sprouts (1/2 green)
- 2 cups of coarsely chopped watercress (1/2 green)

Directions:

1. Combine ½ teaspoon of both pepper and salt, 1 teaspoon of lime juice, and 2 teaspoons of oil in a small bowl. Then brush the mahi-mahi fillets all through with the olive oil mixture.

2. Grill the mahi-mahi on medium-high heat until it becomes done in about 5 minutes, turn it to the other side, and let it be done for about 5 minutes. (You will have an internal temperature of about 145°F).

3. For the slaw, combine the watercress, cucumber, jicama, and alfalfa sprouts in a bowl. Now combine ½ teaspoon of both pepper and salt, 2 teaspoons of lime juice, and 2 tablespoons of extra virgin oil in a small bowl. Drizzle it over slaw and toss together to combine.

Nutrition:

- 320 Calories
- 44g Protein
- 11g Fat

Shrimp Cobb Salad

Difficulty: Easy

Preparation Time: 25 minutes

Cooking Time: 10 minutes

Servings: 2

Ingredients:

- 4 slices center-cut bacon (1 lean)
- 1 lb. large shrimp, peeled and deveined (1 lean)
- 1/2 teaspoon ground paprika (1/8 condiment)
- 1/4 teaspoon ground black pepper (1/8 condiment)
- 1/4 teaspoon salt, divided (1/8 condiment)
- 2 1/2 tablespoons. Fresh lemon juice (1/4 condiment)
- 1 1/2 tablespoons. Extra-virgin olive oil (1/4 condiment)
- 1/2 teaspoon whole grain Dijon mustard (1/4 condiment)
- 1 (10 oz.) package romaine lettuce hearts, chopped (2 green)
- 2 cups cherry tomatoes, quartered (1 green)
- 1 ripe avocado, cut into wedges (1 healthy fat)
- 1 cup shredded carrots (1 green)

Directions:

1. Cook the bacon for 4 minutes on each side in a large skillet over medium heat till crispy.

2. Take away from the skillet and place on paper towels; let cool for 5 minutes. Break the bacon into bits. Throw out most of the bacon fat, leaving behind only 1 tablespoon. in the skillet. Bring the skillet back to medium-high heat. Add black pepper and paprika to the shrimp for seasoning. Cook the shrimp for around 2 minutes on each side until it is opaque. Sprinkle with 1/8 teaspoon of salt for seasoning.

3. Combine the remaining 1/8 teaspoon of salt, mustard, olive oil and lemon juice together in a small bowl. Stir in the romaine hearts.

4. On each serving plate, place 1 and 1/2 cups of romaine lettuce. Add on top the same amounts of avocado, carrots, tomatoes, shrimp and bacon.

Nutrition:

- 528 Calories
- 29g Fat
- 49g Protein

Asparagus and Smoked Salmon Salad

Difficulty: Average

Preparation Time: 15 minutes

Cooking Time: 10 minutes

Servings: 8

Ingredients:

- 1 lb. fresh asparagus, shaped and cut into 1-inch pieces (1 green)
- 1/2 cup pecans, smashed into pieces (1/4 healthy fat)
- 2 heads red leaf lettuce, washed and split (1 green)
- 1/4 lb. smoked salmon, cut into 1-inch chunks (1 lean)
- 1/4 cup olive oil (1/4 condiment)
- 2 tablespoons. lemon juice (1/4 condiment)
- 1 teaspoon Dijon mustard (1/4 condiment)
- 1/2 teaspoon salt (1/4 condiment)
- 1/4 teaspoon pepper (1/4 condiment)

Directions:

1. Boil a pot of water. Stir in asparagus and cook for 5 minutes until tender. Let it drain; set aside.

2. In a skillet, cook the pecans over medium heat for 5 minutes, stirring constantly until lightly toasted.

3. Combine the asparagus, toasted pecans, salmon, and red leaf lettuce and toss in a large bowl.

4. In another bowl, combine lemon juice, pepper, Dijon mustard, salt, and olive oil. You can coat the salad with the dressing or serve it on its side.

Nutrition:

- 159 Calories
- 13g Fat
- 6g Protein

Romaine Lettuce and Radicchios Mix

Difficulty: Easy

Preparation Time: 6 minutes

Cooking Time: 0 minutes

Servings: 4

Ingredients:

- 2 tablespoons olive oil (1/4 condiment)
- A pinch of salt and black pepper (1/4 condiment)
- 2 spring onions, chopped (1 green)
- 3 tablespoons Dijon mustard (1/4 condiment)
- Juice of 1 lime (1/4 condiment)
- ½ cup basil, chopped (1/4 green)
- 4 cups romaine lettuce heads, chopped (2 green)
- 3 radicchios, sliced (1 healthy fat)

Directions:

1. In a salad bowl, blend the lettuce with the spring onions and the other ingredients, toss and serve.

Nutrition:

- 87 Calories
- 2g Fats
- 2g Protein

Coconut-Crusted Chicken Salad

Difficulty: Average

Preparation Time: 9 minutes

Cooking Time: 15 minutes

Servings: 3

Ingredients

For the Vinaigrette:

- 1 tablespoon of extra virgin olive oil (1/4 condiment)
- 1 tablespoon of honey (1/4 condiment)
- A spoonful of white vinegar (1/4 condiment)
- 2 teaspoons Dijon mustard (1/8 condiment)

For the Chicken Salad:

- 6 tablespoons shredded coconut without sweetening (1 healthy fat)
- ¼ cup panko breadcrumbs (1/4 healthy fat)
- 2 tablespoons crushed cornflakes (1/4 healthy fat)
- Salt and black chili pepper, to taste (1/4 condiment)
- Egg whites, lightly beaten, or ½ cup liquid egg white replace (1/4 healthy fat)
- 1 (6-ounce) boneless, skinless breast of chicken, trimmed in fat (1 lean)
- 6 cups mixed greens for babies (2 green)
- ¾ cup scrambled carrots (1/4 green)
- 1 sliced cucumber (1/4 green)
- 1 sliced tomato (1/4 green)

Directions:

1. Preheat the oven to 375°F. Line a parchment-papered baking sheet. Whisk the oil, sugar, vinegar, and mustard together in a small cup. Mix the coconut, panko, cornflakes, salt, and pepper into a small, shallow bowl. Put egg whites in another bowl big enough to suit the chicken and beat them with a fork gently.

2. Season the chicken with salt and pepper. Tuck chicken in egg whites followed by a coconut-panko mixture, pressing coconut mixture on the chicken with your fingers if necessary. Place the chicken on the prepared baking sheet, coat lightly with spray, and bake for 15 minutes. Flip the chicken and bake until gently cooked, about some 10 to 15 minutes.

3. Add 3 cups of baby greens to each platter to serve. Top with onions, tomatoes, and

cucumber. Slice the chicken diagonally and equally split between the salads. Drizzle and cover up.

Nutrition

- 491 calories
- 34g fat
- 21g protein

Mozzarella Radish Salad

Difficulty: Easy

Preparation Time: 10 minutes

Cooking Time: 20 minutes

Servings: 2

Ingredients:

- 8 oz. radish (1 green)
- 4 oz. Mozzarella (1/2 healthy fat)
- 1 teaspoon balsamic vinegar (1/8 condiment)
- ½ teaspoon salt (1/8 condiment)
- 1 tablespoon olive oil (1/8 condiment)
- 1 teaspoon dried oregano (1/8 green)

Directions:

1. Wash the radish carefully and cut it into halves.

2. Preheat the air fryer to 360 F.

3. Put the radish halves in the air fryer basket.

4. Sprinkle the radish with salt and olive oil.

5. Cook the radish for 20 minutes.

6. Shake the radish after 10 minutes of cooking.

7. When the time is over – transfer the radish to the serving plate.

8. Chop Mozzarella roughly.

9. Sprinkle the radish with Mozzarella, balsamic vinegar, and dried oregano.

10. Stir it gently with the help of 2 forks.

11. Serve it immediately.

Nutrition:

- 241 Calories
- 17g Fat
- 17g Protein

Loaded Caesar Salad with Crunchy Chickpeas

Difficulty: Average

Preparation Time: 5 minutes

Cooking Time: 20 minutes

Servings: 6

Ingredients:

For the chickpeas

- 2 (15-ounce) cans chickpeas, drained and rinsed (1 healthy fat)
- 2 tablespoons extra-virgin olive oil (1/8 condiment)
- 1 teaspoon kosher salt (1/8 condiment)
- 1 teaspoon garlic powder (1/8 condiment)
- 1 teaspoon onion powder (1/8 condiment)
- 1 teaspoon dried oregano (1/8 green)

For the dressing

- ½ cup mayonnaise (1/8 healthy fat)
- 2 tablespoons grated Parmesan cheese (1/4 healthy fat)
- 2 tablespoons freshly squeezed lemon juice (1/8 condiment)
- 1 clove garlic, peeled and smashed (1/8 condiment)
- 1 teaspoon Dijon mustard (1/8 condiment)
- ½ tablespoon Worcestershire sauce (1/8 condiment)
- ½ tablespoon anchovy paste (1/2 healthy fat)

For the salad

- 3 heads romaine lettuce, cut into bite-size pieces (1 green)

Directions:

To make the chickpeas

1. Preheat the oven to 450°F. Line a baking sheet with parchment paper.

2. Add the chickpeas, oil, salt, garlic powder, onion powder, and oregano in a small container. Scatter the coated chickpeas on the prepared baking sheet.

3. Roast for about 20 minutes, tossing occasionally, until the chickpeas are golden and have a bit of crunch.

To make the dressing

4.   In a small bowl, whisk the mayonnaise, Parmesan, lemon juice, garlic, mustard, Worcestershire sauce, and anchovy paste until combined.

To make the salad

5.   Combine the lettuce and dressing in a large container. Toss to coat. Top with the roasted chickpeas and serve.

Cooking Tip: Don't wash out that bowl you used for the chickpeas —the remaining oil adds a great punch of flavor to blanched green beans or another simply cooked vegetable.

Nutrition:

- 367 Calories
- 22g Total fat
- 12g Protein

Protein Salad with Buttermilk Dressing

Difficulty: Average

Preparation Time: 11 minutes

Cooking Time: 6 minutes

Servings: 3

Ingredients

- 2 cups spring baby mix (1 green)
- 2 chopped scallions (1 green)
- 1 small, halved, sliced cucumber (1 green)
- 4 mushrooms with white buttons half-cut and sliced (2 healthy fat)
- ¼ medium avocado, chopped and peeled (1/2 healthy fat)
- ½ cup cottage cheese 2 percent (1/2 healthy fat)
- 1 hard-boiled egg, chopped and peeled (1/4 healthy fat)
- 3 tablespoons of low-fat buttermilk (1/4 healthy fat)
- 1 lemon juice (1/8 condiment)
- 1 clove of garlic, chopped (1/8 condiment)
- Salt and black chili pepper, to taste (1/8 condiment)

Direction

1.   Put the spring mixture, scallions, cucumber, mushrooms, avocado, cottage cheese, and egg into a medium bowl.

2.   Stir in buttermilk, lemon juice, garlic, salt, and pepper in a small bowl. Combine using a fork.

3.   Drizzle over the salad, toss and serve.

Nutrition:

- 491 calories
- 38g fat
- 19g protein

Avocado Lime Shrimp Salad

Difficulty: Easy

Preparation Time: 15 minutes

Cooking Time: 0 minutes

Servings: 2

Ingredients:

- 14 ounces of jumbo cooked shrimp, peeled and deveined; chopped (2 lean)
- 4 ½ ounces of avocado, diced (1 healthy fat)
- 1 ½ cup of tomato, diced (1/2 healthy fat)
- ¼ cup of chopped green onion (1/4 green)
- ¼ cup of jalapeno with the seeds removed, diced fine (1/4 green)
- 1 teaspoon of olive oil (1/8 condiment)
- 2 tablespoons of lime juice (1/4 condiment)
- 1/8 teaspoon of salt (1/8 condiment)
- 1 tablespoon of chopped cilantro (1/8 green)

Directions:

1.   Get a small bowl and combine green onion, olive oil, lime juice, pepper, a pinch of salt. Wait for about 5 minutes for all of them to marinate and mellow the flavor of the onion.

2.   Get a large bowl and combine chopped shrimp, tomato, avocado, jalapeno. Combine all of the ingredients, add cilantro, and gently toss.

3.   Add pepper and salt as desired.

Nutrition:

- 314 Calories
- 26g Protein
- 9g Fiber

Cobb Salad

Difficulty: Easy

Preparation Time: 11 minutes

Cooking Time: 0 minutes

Servings: 2

Ingredients

- 1 thin, cored, and chopped head iceberg lettuce (1 green)
- 8 ounces of boneless, skinless breast of chicken (2 lean)
- 2 hard-boiled, peeled, and chopped eggs (1 healthy fat)
- 2 tomatoes, cut (1 green)
- 1 avocado, peeled, sliced, and pitted (1/2 healthy fat)
- 1 cup of rallied carrots (1 green)
- ¼ cup shredded cheese with low fat, mild cheddar (1/2 healthy fat)
- Salad dressing, such as red wine vinaigrette or cucumber ranch dressing (1 condiment)

Directions:

1. Mix it all in a big bowl and throw. Break into different bowls and serve with your choice of dressing.

Nutrition:

- 410 calories
- 31g fat
- 16g protein

Toast with Smoked Salmon, Herbed Cream Cheese, And Greens

Difficulty: Average

Preparation Time: 10 minutes

Cooking Time: 5 minutes

Servings: 2

Ingredients:

For the herbed cream cheese

- ¼ cup cream cheese, at room temperature (1/4 healthy fat)
- 2 tablespoons chopped fresh flat-leaf parsley (1/4 green)
- 2 tablespoons chopped fresh chives or sliced scallion (1/4 green)
- ½ teaspoon garlic powder (1/4 condiment)
- ¼ teaspoon kosher salt (1/4 condiment)

For the toast

- 2 slices bread (1 healthy fat)
- 4 ounces smoked salmon (2 lean)
- Small handful microgreens or sprouts (1 green)
- 1 tablespoon capers, drained and rinsed (1/4 green)
- ¼ small red onion, very thinly sliced (1/4 condiment)

Directions:

To make the herbed cream cheese

1. In a small container, put together the cream cheese, parsley, chives, garlic powder, and salt. Using a fork, mix until combined. Chill until ready to use.

To make the toast

2. Toast the bread until golden. Spread the herbed cream cheese over each piece of toast, then top with the smoked salmon. Garnish with microgreens, capers, and red onion.

Nutrition:

- 325 calories
- 29g fat
- 17g protein

Vegetables in Air Fryer

Difficulty: Easy

Preparation Time: 20 minutes

Cooking Time: 30 minutes

Servings: 2

Ingredients:

- 2 potatoes (1 healthy fat)
- 1 zucchini (1 green)
- 1 onion (1/4 green)
- 1 red pepper (1/4 green)
- 1 green pepper (1/4 green)

Directions:

1. Cut the potatoes into slices. Cut the onion into rings. Cut the zucchini slices. Cut the peppers into strips.

2. Put all the ingredients in the bowl and add a little salt, ground pepper and some extra virgin olive oil. Mix well. Pass to the basket of the air fryer. Select 160°C (320°F), 30 minutes.

3. Check that the vegetables are to your liking.

- 135 Calories
- 11g Fat
- 4g Protein

Taste of Normandy Salad

Difficulty: Easy
Preparation Time: 25 minutes
Cooking Time: 5 minutes
Servings: 4 to 6
Ingredients:
For the walnuts

- 2 tablespoons butter (1/4 healthy fat)
- ¼ cup sugar or honey (1/8 condiment)
- 1 cup walnut pieces (1/4 healthy fat)
- ½ teaspoon kosher salt (1/8 condiment)

For the dressing

- 3 tablespoons extra-virgin olive oil (1/4 condiment)
- 1½ tablespoons champagne vinegar (1/8 condiment)
- 1½ tablespoons Dijon mustard (1/8 condiment)
- ¼ teaspoon kosher salt (1/8 condiment)

For the salad

- 1 head red leaf lettuce, shredded into pieces (1 green)
- 3 heads endive, ends trimmed and leaves separated (1 green)
- 2 apples, cored and divided into thin wedges (1/2 green)
- 1 (8-ounce) Camembert wheel, cut into thin wedges (1/2 green)

Direction

To make the walnuts

1. Dissolve the butter in a skillet over medium high heat. Stir in the sugar and cook until it dissolves. Add the walnuts and cook for about 5 minutes, stirring until toasty. Season with salt and transfer to a plate to cool.

To make the dressing

2. Whip the oil, vinegar, mustard, and salt in a large bowl until combined.

To make the salad

3. Add the lettuce and endive to the bowl with the dressing and toss to coat. Transfer to a serving platter.

4. Decoratively arrange the apple and Camembert wedges over the lettuce and scatter the walnuts on top. Serve immediately.

Meal Prep Tip: Prepare the walnuts in advance—in fact, double the quantities and use them throughout the week to add a healthy crunch to salads, oats, or simply to enjoy as a snack.

Nutrition:

- 699 Calories
- 52g fat
- 23g Protein

Super Green Salad

Difficulty: Easy
Preparation Time: 10 minutes
Cooking Time: 9 minutes
Servings: 3
Ingredients

- 4 cups of kale chopped (1 green)
- 4 cups of fresh spinach (1 green)
- 3 spoonful of extra virgin olive oil (1/4 condiment)
- 1 cup lemon juice (1/4 condiment)
- Salt and black chili pepper, to taste (1/8 condiment)
- 6 hard-boiled eggs, quartered and peeled (2 healthy fat)
- 2 big, peeled, pitted, and sliced avocado (1 healthy fat)
- 4 tablespoons of Parmesan cheese rubbed (1/2 healthy fat)

Directions:

1. Put the kale, spinach, olive oil, lemon juice, salt, and pepper into a large bowl. Toss the greens to mix, cover with dressing. Divide the salad into 4 slices.

2. Top with chicken and avocado on every bed of greens. Sprinkle with cheese on each salad and serve straight away.

Nutrition:

- 411 calories
- 27g fat
- 11g protein

Dessert Recipes

Chocolate Popsicle

Difficulty: Easy

Preparation Time: 20 minutes

Cooking Time: 10 minutes

Servings: 6

Ingredients:

- 4 oz. unsweetened chocolate, chopped (1 healthy fat)
- 6 drops liquid stevia (1/2 condiment)
- 1 ½ cups heavy cream (1/2 healthy fat)

Directions:

1. Add heavy cream into the microwave-safe bowl and microwave until it just begins boiling.

2. Add chocolate into the heavy cream and set aside for 5 minutes.

3. Add liquid stevia into the heavy cream mixture and stir until chocolate is melted.

4. Pour mixture into the Popsicle molds and place in freezer for 4 hours or until set.

5. Serve and enjoy.

Nutrition:

- 198 Calories
- 21g Fats
- 3g Protein

Vanilla Bean Frappuccino

Difficulty: Easy

Preparation Time: 3 minutes

Cooking Time: 6 minutes

Servings: 4 servings

Ingredients:

- 3 cups unsweetened vanilla almond milk, chilled (1/2 healthy fat)
- 2 tsp. swerve (1/2 condiment)
- 1 ½ cups heavy cream, cold (1/2 healthy fat)
- 1 vanilla bean (1 lean)
- ¼ tsp. xanthan gum (1/2 condiment)

Directions:

1. Combine the almond milk, swerve, heavy cream, vanilla bean, and xanthan gum in the blender and process at high speed for 1 minute until smooth.

2. Pour into tall shake glasses, sprinkle with chocolate shavings, and serve immediately.

Nutrition:

- 193 Calories
- 14g Fats
- 15g Protein

Peanut Butter Coconut Popsicle

Difficulty: Average

Preparation Time: 15 minutes

Cooking Time: 0 minutes

Servings: 12

Ingredients:

- ½ cup peanut butter (1/2 healthy fat)
- 1 tsp. liquid stevia (1/4 condiment)
- 2 cans unsweetened coconut milk (2 healthy fat)

Directions:

1. In the blender, add all the listed ingredients and blend until smooth.

2. Pour mixture into the Popsicle molds and place in the freezer for 4 hours or until set.

3. Serve.

Nutrition:

- 155 Calories
- 15g Fats
- 3g Protein

Chocolate Almond Butter Brownie

Difficulty: Average

Preparation Time: 10 minutes

Cooking Time: 16 minutes

Servings: 4

Ingredients:

- 1 cup bananas, overripe (1 lean)
- ½ cup almond butter, melted (1/2 healthy fat)
- 1 scoop protein powder (1 healthy fat)
- 2 tbsp. unsweetened cocoa powder (1 condiment)

Directions:

1.   Preheat the air fryer to 325°F. Grease air fryer baking pan and set aside.

2.   Blend all ingredients in a blender until smooth.

3.   Pour batter into the prepared pan, and place in the air fryer basket and cook for 16 minutes.

4.   Serve and enjoy.

Nutrition:

*   82 Calories
*   2g Fats
*   7g Protein

Avocado Pudding

Difficulty: Easy

Preparation Time: 20 minutes

Cooking Time: 0 minutes

Servings: 8

Ingredients:

*   2 ripe avocados, pitted and cut into pieces (2 lean)
*   1 tbsp. fresh lime juice (1/4 condiment)
*   14 oz. can coconut milk (1/2 healthy fat)
*   2 tsp. liquid stevia (1/4 condiment)
*   2 tsp. vanilla (1/4 condiment)

Directions:

1.   Inside the blender, add all ingredients and blend until smooth.

2.   Serve immediately and enjoy.

Nutrition:

*   317 Calories
*   30g Fats
*   3g Protein

Dark Chocolate Mochaccino Ice Bombs

Difficulty: Average

Preparation Time: 5 minutes

Cooking Time: 10 minutes

Servings: 4

Ingredients:

*   ½ lb. cream cheese (1 healthy fat)
*   4 tbsp. powdered sweetener (1 condiment)
*   2 oz. strong coffee (1 condiment)
*   2 tbsp. cocoa powder, unsweetened (1 condiment)
*   1 oz. cocoa butter, melted (1/2 healthy fat)
*   2 ½ oz. dark chocolate, melted (1/2 healthy fat)

Directions:

1.   Combine cream cheese, sweetener, coffee, and cocoa powder in a food processor.

2.   Roll 2 tbsp. of the mixture and place on a lined tray.

3.   Mix the melted cocoa butter and chocolate, and coat the bombs with it.

4.   Freeze for 2 hours.

Nutrition:

*   127 Calories
*   13g Fats
*   1.9g Protein

Chocolate Bars

Difficulty: Average

Preparation Time: 10 minutes

Cooking Time: 20 minutes

Servings: 16

Ingredients:

*   15 oz. cream cheese, softened (2 healthy fat)
*   15 oz. unsweetened dark chocolate (2 healthy fat)
*   1 tsp. vanilla (1 condiment)
*   10 drops liquid stevia (2 condiment)

Directions:

1.   Grease an 8-inch square dish and set aside.

2.   In a saucepan, dissolve chocolate over low heat.

3.   Add stevia and vanilla and stir well.

4.   Remove pan from heat and set aside.

5.   Add cream cheese into the blender and blend until smooth.

6.   Add melted chocolate mixture into the cream cheese and blend until just combined.

7.   Transfer mixture into the prepared dish and spread evenly, and place in the refrigerator until firm.

8.   Slice and serve.

Nutrition:

- 230 Calories
- 24g Fats
- 6g Protein

Smooth Peanut Butter Cream

Difficulty: Average

Preparation Time: 10 minutes

Cooking Time: 0 minutes

Servings: 8

Ingredients:

- ¼ cup peanut butter (1/4 healthy fat)
- 4 overripe bananas, chopped (1 lean)
- 1/3 cup cocoa powder (1/2 condiment)
- 1/3 tsp. vanilla extract (1/2 condiment)
- 1/8 tsp. salt (1/8 condiment)

Directions:

1. In the blender, add all the listed ingredients and blend until smooth.
2. Serve immediately and enjoy.

Nutrition:

- 101 Calories
- 5g Fats
- 3g Protein

Vanilla Avocado Popsicles

Difficulty: Easy

Preparation Time: 20 minutes

Cooking Time: 0 minutes

Servings: 6

Ingredients:

- 2 avocadoes (2 lean)
- 1 tsp. vanilla (1/4 condiment)
- 1 cup almond milk (1/2 healthy fat)
- 1 tsp. liquid stevia (1/4 condiment)
- ½ cup unsweetened cocoa powder (1/4 condiment)

Directions:

1. In the blender, add all the listed ingredients and blend smoothly.
2. Pour blended mixture into the Popsicle molds and place in the freezer until set.
3. Serve and enjoy.

Nutrition:

- 130 Calories

- 12g Fats
- 3g Protein

Coconut Coffee and Ghee

Difficulty: Easy

Preparation Time: 10 minutes

Cooking Time: 10 minutes

Servings: 5

Ingredients:

- ½ tbsp. coconut oil (1/2 condiment)
- ½ tbsp. ghee (1/2 condiment)
- 1 to 2 cups preferred coffee (or rooibos or black tea, if preferred) (1 healthy fat)
- 1 tbsp. coconut or almond milk (1/2 healthy fat)

Directions:

1. Place the almond (or coconut) milk, coconut oil, ghee, and coffee in a blender (or milk frothier).
2. Mix for around 10 seconds or until the coffee turns creamy and foamy.
3. Pour contents into a coffee cup.
4. Serve immediately and enjoy.

Nutrition:

- 150 Calories
- 15g Fats
- 0.1g Protein

Chocolate Frosty

Difficulty: Easy

Preparation Time: 20 minutes

Cooking Time: 0 minutes

Servings: 4

Ingredients:

- 2 tbsp. unsweetened cocoa powder (1/2 condiment)
- 1 cup heavy whipping cream (1 healthy fat)
- 1 tbsp. almond butter (1 healthy fat)
- 5 drops liquid stevia (1/4 condiment)
- 1 tsp. vanilla (1/4 condiment)

Directions:

1. Add cream into the medium bowl and beat using the hand mixer for 5 minutes.

2. Add remaining ingredients and blend until thick cream form.

3. Pour in serving bowls and place them in the freezer for 30 minutes.

4. Serve and enjoy.

Nutrition:

- 137 Calories
- 13g Fats
- 2g Protein

Cranberry Salad

Difficulty: Easy

Preparation Time: 5 minutes

Cooking Time: 5 minutes

Servings: 2

Ingredients:

- 1 sugar-free cranberry Jell-O pack, ½ cup for snacks allowed (1/2 healthy fat)
- ½ cup celery chopped, (1 green)
- 7 Half Cut Walnut (1/2 healthy fat)

Directions:

1. Mix Jell-O according to the instructions of the box.

2. Add walnuts and celery.

3. Allow setting.

4. Shake until serving.

5. Distribute servings in 4 ½ cups.

Nutrition:

- 341 calories
- 11g Fats
- 4.1g Protein

Almond Butter Fudge

Difficulty: Average

Preparation Time: 10 minutes

Cooking Time: 10 minutes

Servings: 18

Ingredients:

- ¾ cup creamy almond butter (1 healthy fat)
- 1 ½ cups unsweetened chocolate chips (1 healthy fat)

Directions:

1. Line 8x4-inch pan with parchment paper and set aside.

2. Add chocolate chips and almond butter into the double boiler and cook over medium heat until the chocolate-butter mixture is melted. Stir well.

3. Place mixture into the prepared pan and place in the freezer until set.

4. Slice and serve.

Nutrition:

- 197 Calories
- 16g Fats
- 4g Protein

Mousse

Difficulty: Average

Preparation Time: 3 minutes

Cooking Time: 3 minutes

Servings: 2

Ingredients:

- 1 Medifast or Optavia hot cocoa packet (1 condiment)
- ½ cup sugar-free gelatin (1 condiment)
- 1 tbsp. light cream cheese (1/2 healthy fat)
- 2 tbsp. cold water (1/2 condiment)
- ¼ cup crushed ice (1/2 condiment)

Directions:

1. Place all ingredients in a blender.

2. Pulse until smooth.

3. Pour into glass and place in the fridge to set.

4. Serve chilled.

Nutrition:

- 156 Calories
- 3.7g Fat
- 5.7g Protein

Peanut Butter Fudge

Difficulty: Average

Preparation Time: 10 minutes

Cooking Time: 10 minutes

Servings: 20

Ingredients:

- ¼ cup almonds, toasted and chopped (1 healthy fat)

- 12 oz. smooth peanut butter (1/2 healthy fat)
- 15 drops liquid stevia (1/2 condiment)
- 3 tbsp. coconut oil (1/2 healthy fat)
- 4 tbsp. coconut cream (1/2 healthy fat)

Directions:

1. Line baking tray with parchment paper.

2. Melt coconut oil in a pan over low heat. Add peanut butter, coconut cream, stevia, and salt in a saucepan. Stir well.

3. Pour fudge mixture into the prepared baking tray and sprinkle chopped almonds on top.

4. Place the tray in the refrigerator for 1 hour or until set.

5. Slice and serve.

Nutrition:

- 131 Calories
- 12g Fats
- 5g Protein

Peanut Butter Brownie and Ice Cream Sandwiches

Difficulty: Easy

Preparation Time: 2 minutes

Cooking Time: 2 minutes

Servings: 2

Ingredients:

- 1 Medifast Brownie Mix packet (1 condiment)
- 3 tbsp. water (1 condiment)
- 1 Peanut Butter Crunch Bar or any bar of your choice (1 healthy fat)
- 2 tbsp. peanut butter powder (2 healthy fat)
- 1 tbsp. water (1 condiment)
- 2 tbsp. cool whip (1 healthy fat)

Directions:

1. Melt the Brownie Mix with water.

2. Add in the Peanut Butter Crunch until a dough is formed.

3. Spoon 4 dough balls on a plate and flatten using the palm of your hands.

4. Make sure that the dough is ¼ inch thick.

5. Place in a microwave oven and cook for 2 minutes.

6. Meanwhile, mix the Peanut Butter Powder and water to form a paste.

7. Add cool whip. Set aside in the fridge to chill for at least 1 hour.

8. Take the cookies out from the microwave oven and allow them to cool.

9. Once cooled, spoon the Peanut Butter ice cream in between two cookies.

10. Serve immediately.

Nutrition:

- 410 Calories
- 13.2g Fat
- 8.3g Protein

Raspberry Ice Cream

Difficulty: Easy

Preparation Time: 10 minutes

Cooking Time: 0 minutes

Servings: 2

Ingredients:

- 1 cup frozen raspberries (1 lean)
- ½ cup heavy cream (1/2 healthy fat)
- 1/8 tsp. stevia powder (1/8 condiment)

Directions:

1. Blend all the listed ingredients in a blender until smooth.

2. Serve immediately and enjoy.

Nutrition:

- 144 Calories
- 11g Fats
- 2g Protein

Chocolate Bark with Almonds

Difficulty: Average

Preparation Time: 5 minutes

Cooking Time: 10 minutes

Servings: 12

Ingredients:

- ½ cup toasted almonds, chopped (1/2 healthy fat)
- ½ cup butter (1 healthy fat)
- 10 drops stevia (1 condiment)
- ¼ tsp. salt (1/2 condiment)

- ½ cup unsweetened coconut flakes (1/2 healthy fat)
- 4 oz. dark chocolate (1/2 healthy fat)

Directions:

1. Melt together the butter and chocolate in the microwave for 90 seconds.

2. Remove and stir in stevia.

3. Line a cookie sheet with waxed paper and spread the chocolate evenly.

4. Scatter the almonds and coconut flakes on top, and sprinkle with salt.

5. Refrigerate for one hour.

Nutrition:

- 161 Calories
- 15.3g Fats
- 1.9g Protein

Blueberry Muffins

Difficulty: Average
Preparation Time: 15 minutes
Cooking Time: 35 minutes
Servings: 12
Ingredients:

- 2 eggs (2 lean)
- ½ cup fresh blueberries (1 healthy fat)
- 1 cup heavy cream (1 healthy fat)
- 2 cups almond flour (1/2 condiment)
- ¼ tsp. lemon zest (1/4 condiment)
- ½ tsp. lemon extract (1/4 condiment)
- 1 tsp. baking powder (1/8 condiment)
- 5 drops stevia (1/4 condiment)
- ¼ cup butter, melted (1/4 healthy fat)

Directions:

1. Heat the cooker to 350°F. Line muffin tin with cupcake liners and set aside.

2. Add eggs into the bowl and whisk until mixed.

3. Add remaining ingredients and mix to combine.

4. Pour mixture into the prepared muffin tin and bake for 25 minutes.

5. Serve and enjoy.

Nutrition:

- 190 Calories
- 17g Fats
- 10g Protein

No Bake Fueling Peanut Butter Brownies

Difficulty: Average
Preparation Time: 5 minutes
Cooking Time: 30 minutes
Servings: 6
Ingredients:

- 3 tbsp. peanut butter (2 healthy fat)
- 1 cup water (1 condiment)
- 6 Optavia Double Chocolate Brownie Fueling packets (3 condiment)

Directions:

1. Put all ingredients in a bowl and mix until all elements are well incorporated.

2. Pour into silicone molds and place in the freezer.

3. Freeze for 30 minutes before eating.

Nutrition:

- 906 Calories
- 32g Fats
- 9g Protein

Conclusion

Cooking in an air fryer is an awesome way to cook food. Wheat flour breaded fish can be easily prepared in an air fryer, which results in crispy crusts and juicy insides. People on a diet should opt for air frying as it prepares food without frying and reduces the oil content by half. Air frying vegetable strips away the vegetable's excess water, which makes the vegetable delicious and tasty. Using this with your Lean and green diet is a great help. To make the diet much easier, you will be glad to know that lean and green food can be used along with air frying to make the diet much easier.

The Lean and Green diet is a diet which claims to be the healthiest and environmentally sustainable. It is also a diet which has good weight loss and muscle building properties.

The Lean and Green Diet is based on these principles: A predominantly plant-based diet with an emphasis on vegetables, fruits, whole grains and beans. A high level of physical activity (at least 30 minutes of aerobic exercise 3 times a week). Adherence to the nutritional recommendations from governmental food agencies (WCRF/AICR). Lastly, increased consumption of fish, poultry, whole-grains and low-fat dairy products (in the case of vegetarians). These 4 principles present a total package which promises to allow for the identification, identification and implementation of an effective lifestyle change. However, as with many other diets, the Lean and Green Diet has not been rigorously tested and thus it is often difficult to find scientific evidence for the diet's effectiveness.

However, there is scientific evidence for one of the principles: an environmental approach to food. For example, the use of recycled packaging at supermarkets could reduce a consumer's carbon footprint by 5-10%, according to the University of British Columbia. This is in comparison to the use of environmentally unfriendly packaging. There can also be environmental gains from reduced packaging from suppliers. For example, Anheuser-Busch uses windmills to reduce its energy usage by 25% and reduce the amount of carbon dioxide released into the atmosphere by 9%.

In relation to this, a key principle of Lean and Green is that it must be environmentally sustainable. It is often suggested that consumers take advantage of their purchasing power and bring about a change in the food system.

At this moment of your journey, you must recognize that you've overcome the hardest task, i.e., the first dreadful step towards health and wellbeing. Please remember that this alone is a commendable feat and whoever survives the first step can survive the rest and come out at the other side thinner, stronger, wiser, happier, and overall better.

Remember, the journey of a thousand miles still begins with just a single step indeed. So, stand tall, be confident, and just go ahead each day with your ideal vision of yourself in your mind, moving a bit closer to your goals every day.

The program has earned worldwide acclaim for its ability to deliver sustainable results without complicating people's meal program. It places very few food restrictions and inspires people to choose a healthier version of their daily food without compromising on taste and nutrition.